Jane Atkinson's book can be commended on relating to God is at the heart of what pray Christian offers a refreshing angle for exploring the Gospel material. She offers a very practical directed study which, using a basically Ignatian approach, takes participants smoothly into their own personal engagement with God. The notes on using the studies explain well how the various sections are intended to work together, providing an important balance between the objective and the subjective. While valuable for individual use, the book comes into its own in a group setting, with its potential for shared engagement.

—**REV DR JOHN NOLLAND BSC, THL, BD, PHD.** RETIRED LECTURER IN NEW TESTAMENT STUDIES AT TRINITY THEOLOGICAL COLLEGE, BRISTOL AND PREVIOUSLY REGENT COLLEGE, VANCOUVER.

Jane Atkinson deals with 47 profound lessons on the father heart of God in a readable and practical way in this book. In a trial run of the sessions a group of us studied all of them, experiencing incredible benefits in our lives as we spent time thinking, imagining, praying and interacting with the characters/incidents. The icing on the cake is the author's vivid description of the historical, geographical and cultural background to the events. Each study provides new insights and experiences as each incident is different, while the main focus is on Jesus' responses, which helped people to receive what they needed and enabled them to draw closer to God. The author has brought out this invaluable book with much prayer and I highly recommend it to anyone who desires spiritual growth, as it facilitates a deeper understanding of the father heart of God, as seen in Jesus.

—**LOIS MEDIKONDA**. CO-FOUNDER OF PARTNERSHIP INDIA WITH HER HUSBAND KRISHNAIAH MEDIKONDA, EQUIPPING CHURCH LEADERS BY PROVIDING COUNSEL, SUPPORT, TRAINING AND TEACHING OF GOD'S WORD.

It is not easy to describe this book, *God's Heart for Answering Prayer*, because it does not fit into any of the usual categories of books on prayer, but neither is it a biblical commentary on the Gospels. What Jane Atkinson has given to us is a treasure of meditations upon the ministry of Jesus which sheds fresh light upon his relationships with his disciples, his family and friends, the sick and the needy, as well as others whom he encountered. The author's own personal relationship with Jesus shines through this study and she uses her practical experience to bring a fresh perspective on prayer that even the most mature of Christians will find helpful. As a Lenten study for groups or personal use I warmly commend this book.

—**REV DR CLIFFORD HILL MA. BD. PHD.**

Delving into Jane Atkinson's book was thrilling and electrifying, as she lights up the Gospel narrative about people meeting with Jesus. Her searching questions pose exciting challenges. Jane introduced sessions for our Bible Study Group, guiding us in probing reasons for Christ's responses when engaging with characters whose motives He knew. Wondering at Jesus' compassionate humility, always obedient to His Father's will, we also pondered Jane's touching phrase "the Father's heart" as each session unfolded, showing our Father God's "extravagant" love. Background verses indicate the context and atmosphere while Jane's reading and re-reading of chosen passages, followed by a pause, let us select a character to identify with, giving us greater awareness of the reality of what had happened and the dramatic effects on lives touched, plus a uniquely beautiful, shared experience of Jesus. Immersing yourself in this book will lead you to a stronger relationship with our Father God.

—**JANICE G. LUFF.** RETIRED HOSPITAL NURSE.

Jane Atkinson knows her Bible and I found her work insightful and scholarly. In these studies she helps us to realize how much we can learn about the nature of God the Father from looking at the life of Jesus; his responses to people and his relationships can help us to understand the Father in a way that illuminates His character. I think any Christian would benefit from following these studies, whether in a small group setting or individually as an aid to private prayer.

—**SALLY HOGG.** BIBLE STUDY GROUP LEADER, MEETING ON ZOOM.
RETIRED SOCIAL SERVICES MANAGER AND CIVIL SERVANT.
AUTHOR OF *INVISIBLE WOMEN: A HISTORY OF WOMEN IN THE CHURCH.*

GOD'S HEART
FOR ANSWERING
PRAYER

**FOR USE INDIVIDUALLY OR IN GROUPS,
DAILY THROUGH LENT OR WEEKLY THROUGH THE YEAR**

GOD'S HEART
FOR ANSWERING
PRAYER

47 BIBLE STUDY OUTLINES
TO HELP YOU PRAY

J.H. ATKINSON

God's Heart for Answering Prayer
Copyright © 2024 J.H.Atkinson
All rights reserved

No part of this book may be reproduced in any form or by any electronic or mechanical means, including information storage and retrieval systems, or transmitted in any form by any means, electronic, mechanical, photocopying, recording or otherwise, without prior written permission from the author, except for the use of brief quotations in a book review.

The right of J. H. Atkinson to be identified as the author of this work has been asserted by her in accordance with the Copyright, Designs and Patents Act 1988.

British Library Cataloguing in Publication Data:
a catalogue record for this publication is available from the British Library.

Unless otherwise indicated, all Scripture quotations are taken from the World English Bible, (Public Domain).

Scripture quotations marked NLT are taken from the *Holy Bible*, New Living Translation, copyright © 1996, 2004, 2015 by Tyndale House Foundation. Used by permission of Tyndale House Publishers, Inc., Carol Stream, Illinois 60188. All rights reserved.

ISBN: 978-1-0685558-0-0 (Paperback)   978-1-0685558-1-7 (e-Book)

Published in the UK in 2025 by Prosferro Press, Bristol
https://www.prosferropress.com

Front cover image: Masada by vvvita
Book designed by: Mark Karis

This study guide is dedicated to

Janice Luff, Lois Medikonda, Margaret Webb,
Sally Hogg and Wendy Gazeley,

who faithfully took part in a trial week by week and whose participation prompted inclusion of the Context and Meditation sections and many more questions than originally planned.

With grateful thanks for all the encouragement!

CONTENTS

Introduction 1

PART 1. JESUS AND FATHER GOD 11

1   Jesus' Baptism. Matthew 3:13-17 13

2   "I Thank You, Father, Lord of Heaven and Earth." Matthew 11:20-30 19

3   Raising of Lazarus. John 11:38-44 26

4   Jesus' Prayer for His Followers. John 17:1-26 33

5   Jesus in Gethsemane. Matthew 26:36-46 39

6   Death of Jesus. Matthew 27:45-56 46

PART 2. JESUS AND HIS FAMILY 53

7   Jesus' Parents when He was Twelve Years Old. Luke 2:41-52 55

8   Jesus' Second Cousin, John the Baptist. Matthew 11:2-15 61

9   Jesus' Mother and Brothers. Matthew 12:46-50 66

10 Jesus' Neighbours in Nazareth. Matthew 13:53-58 71

11 Jesus' Brothers. John 7:1-10 76

12 Mary, the Mother of Jesus, at the Cross. John 19:25-27 81

PART 3. JESUS AND HIS DISCIPLES 87

13   "Save Us, Lord! We Are Dying!" Matthew 8:23-27 89

14   "Why Do You Speak To Them In Parables?" Matthew 13:10-23 94

15   "Lord, It Is Good For Us To Be Here. If You Want,
Let's Make Three Tents." Matthew 17:1-13 101

16   "Why Weren't We Able To Cast It Out?" Matthew 17:14-21 107

17   "Who then is Greatest in the Kingdom of Heaven?" Matthew 18:1-9 111

18   "Lord, How Often Shall My Brother Sin Against Me, and I Forgive Him?"
Matthew 18:21-35 118

19   "Command That These, My Two Sons, May Sit, One on Your Right Hand
and One on Your Left Hand, in Your Kingdom." Matthew 20:20-28 123

20   "Lord, Don't You Care that My Sister Left Me to Serve Alone?
Ask Her therefore to Help Me." Luke 10:38-42 128

21   "How Did the Fig Tree Immediately Wither Away?" Matthew 21:18-22 133

22   "Why This Waste?" Matthew 26:6-13 140

PART 4. JESUS AND THE SICK AND NEEDY 145

23   A Leper and a Roman Centurion. Matthew 8:1-13 147

24   Demoniacs and Pigs. Matthew 8:28-34 153

25   Jairus's Daughter Raised from the Dead and
a Woman's Haemorrhage Healed. Matthew 9:18-26 158

26   Two Blind Men and a Dumb Man Healed. Matthew 9: 27-34 162

27   Canaanite Woman's Daughter Healed. Matthew 15:21-28 167

28   Two Blind Men Near Jericho. Matthew 20:29-34 175

29   The Raising of Lazarus. John 11:17-44 180

PART 5. JESUS, RELIGIOUS LEADERS AND RELUCTANT FOLLOWERS ... 187

30 Leave Home and Family. Matthew 8:18-22 ... 189

31 The Pharisees' Response to Jesus Forgiving a Paralytic. Matthew 9:1-8 ... 194

32 Jesus, Lord of the Sabbath. Matthew 12:1-14 ... 198

33 Ceremonial and Real Defilement. Matthew 15:1-20 ... 203

34 Demand for a Sign. Matthew 16:1-12 ... 209

35 Divorce. Matthew 19:3-12 ... 214

36 A Rich Young Man. Matthew 19:16-30 ... 219

37 Payment of Taxes. Matthew 22:15-22 ... 225

38 Debate on Resurrection. Matthew 22:23-33 ... 230

39 The Great Commandment. Matthew 22:34-46 ... 234

PART 6. JESUS, THE CIVIC AUTHORITIES AND THE CROSS ... 239

40 Mary of Bethany Anointing Jesus with Perfume.
    Matthew 26:6-13 and John 12:1-8 ... 241

41 Judas. Matthew 26:47-56 ... 248

42 Caiaphas. Matthew 26:57-68 ... 254

43 Pilate. John 18:33-38 and 19:4-16 ... 259

44 The Roman Soldiers. Matthew 27:27-31 and 50-54 ... 266

45 John and Mary, the Mother of Jesus. John 19:25-27 ... 271

46 The Criminals Crucified with Jesus. Luke 23:32-43 ... 276

47 Mary Magdalene and the Other Mary Meet the Risen Jesus.
    Matthew 27:57-61 and 28:1-10 ... 281

About the Author ... 288

Notes ... 289

INTRODUCTION

The author once heard a sermon on prayer designed to answer the question: "Does God answer prayer?" The answer given was "Yes," but that it may not always seem like it if God's answer is "No" or "Wait." Exploring the idea that Jesus provides us with a window into the heart of Father God for answering prayer quickly led to the recognition that there is way more to prayer than answers in the form of "Yes," "No," or "Wait." What stood out was that not only was Jesus aware of what was going on in the hearts of those around Him without them needing to say anything, but that He was also wanting to be known by those who were willing to follow Him. His meeting with Nathanael recorded in John 1:43-51 provides an example. Nathanael was not hoping for much on account of his prejudice against Nazareth. He was astonished when Jesus turned out to know more about him than He could ever have been told, to the point where he recognized who Jesus was immediately.

One of Jesus' aims was authentic relationships to the point of intimacy. That presupposes maturity. The "Yes," "No," "Wait" scenario started to look very like the equivalent of a small child asking Daddy for an ice cream. That, of course, is a very important stage in the journey to maturity, as through it one learns to depend on one's parents and to trust, to ask and to accept the reply, whether or not the ice cream is forthcoming. After all, there are many reasons for being denied one! However, no good parent wants to see their child stuck in that phase of their development. The aim is that they should grow up able to become independent and to form healthy, other centred relationships. Jesus was past master!

Jesus once said to Philip that because Philip had seen Him, he had effectively seen the Father, as Jesus was one with Him (John 14:8-10).

It follows that if we consider Jesus' responses to those who came to Him with their comments and requests, we have a window into the Father heart of God for responding to our prayers, on the basis that Jesus is God, so those who came to Him and instigated conversation were praying, even if they did not recognize it themselves at the time.

Jesus was approached by many different people, who between them had a wide range of agendas. His responses were equally wide ranging. His relationship with His immediate blood family was quite different from that with his close friends and followers, whom He designated as His true family. He showed unwavering compassion to those who came to Him out of a sense of need and to women, in contrast with His responses to the religious authorities, which were aimed at bringing them to repentance. All of these people were human, as are all of us. Much as we might like to find ourselves identifying predominantly with Jesus' close friends, in fact we might well find that some of the interactions of others with Jesus also resonate with us, rather uncomfortably at times. Furthermore, it is impossible to consider Jesus purely in terms of His reflection of Father God. He was also a human being and as such modelled for us what our relationship with Father God could look like. This provides a starting point for our journey into understanding prayer more deeply. The first half a dozen sessions focus on Jesus' own relationship with Father God, before moving on to look at different groups of people, including Jesus' blood family, His disciples, sick and suffering who came to Him for help and healing and the religious leaders. The last of the six Parts, focussing on the civic authorities, includes representatives from all those other groups of people, who interacted with Jesus during the last week of His life.

No amount of theoretical understanding about prayer can substitute for actually praying. It is through the practice of prayer that we start to get to know God for ourselves. As well as inviting thought or discussion about how Jesus and by implication the Father responded to those who came to Him, the Bible Study outlines presented here also invite us to come to Him in prayer ourselves. We can do this by reading the Bible

INTRODUCTION

passage under consideration very slowly and imagining ourselves as part of the scene. This can be done by identifying with one of the characters or being ourselves as an additional character present to the events. It can be very interesting to see what unfolds between us and the others who were there, especially Jesus. It can also be very instructive, and we can learn surprising things about our attitudes and responses to Him. It is about allowing the Scriptures to read us having first read them. This can be done in a group, with subsequent sharing if anyone present would like to tell the group what happened in the silence. Safety boundaries are advised for this process, including no sharing of anyone else's contribution outside the group and no comments on what anyone else has shared.

There are forty-seven Sessions in all, lending themselves to weekly group meetings for the best part of a year or to use by individuals on a daily basis during Lent, commencing on Ash Wednesday and ending on Easter Day, or indeed at any other time of year. The discussion questions and comments on each passage are designed to aid understanding prior to praying the passage.

NOTES ON USING THE SESSIONS, ESPECIALLY FOR GROUP LEADERS

During a trial of all the sessions with a group of six people, an hour was found to be a comfortable length of time to cover all the sections. That said, sometimes the Comments were left unread and the Observation section did not yet exist, it appeared week by week, as the fruit of the meditations during the trial. With a group larger than six people it is likely that a longer time will be required for each session, to allow for more people to make contributions and to prevent the Meditation section from becoming rushed.

CONTEXT

Each session begins with a paragraph or two describing what has been taking place in Jesus' life prior to the event that is the focus of the session.

In a group setting it is designed to be read out loud to the group at the start of the session, to remind those who already know and to help those who may not be so familiar with Jesus' life.

PASSAGE REFERENCE
The passage is designed to be read out loud in the group after reading the Context section. For convenience all the passages are included, but as part of the Meditation section, in order to reduce the need to turn pages during the meditation. All the passages and other biblical quotations, are taken from the World English Bible (WEB), which is an update of the American Standard Version and is in the public domain. It can be found on Bible Gateway, where the underlined references act as live links. They are best omitted when reading the passage during the meditation. The language reflects the original Greek sentence construction quite closely. If preferred, any version of the Bible can be used, both for reading the passage at the beginning of each session and for the meditation.

QUESTIONS FOR THOUGHT OR DISCUSSION
During a trial of the sessions with a group of six people, the discussion normally lasted for about forty five minutes. The questions are designed to lead people to draw conclusions for themselves before discovering that they are then summarized in the Comments. That way people are more likely to make meaning and to remember what they have learned. The trial began with about four questions per session, but it quickly became apparent that having so few questions took too much for granted, even in a group of people who all know their Bibles well. The increased number of questions now being presented is with a view to facilitating a gradual unpacking of each passage, bit by bit. Any questions that are unhelpful can be omitted and sometimes it will be necessary to rephrase the question or to add additional ones as the discussion develops. The aim is not to tell people, but to help them to work it out for themselves. At an early stage people that were involved in the trial started asking for the passage reference

and the questions in advance, so that they could think about the questions and prepare for their input to the group beforehand. This will take care of itself when all group members have a copy of this book. One of the group members regularly referred to the internet for help with answering the questions and brought some very interesting and helpful contributions to the group sessions as a result.

COMMENTS

The Comments section is intended as a summary of what has been discussed. In every case it was written before the questions were devised, in order to provide a focus for the questions. It is recommended that in a group setting the leader reads the Comments in advance as part of the preparation for leading the session. This will mean that should additional questions prove necessary the leader will know where they need to lead. Whether or not group members do the same is up to them. It may well be that they will benefit more by not reading the Comments beforehand, although people who are unfamiliar with the Gospels might find it helpful to read the Comments in advance. In the trial the Comments were not shared with group members until after the discussion and were then used as a summary of what had been discussed. If time was short they were omitted, in order to ensure that there was time for the Meditation, which was never omitted.

MEDITATION

Just as learning about how to drive a car from a manual is no substitute for getting into a car and trying to drive it, so learning about God and discussing prayer is not the same thing as getting to know God personally. To do that requires that we learn to interact with God ourselves and pray, rather than to stop at talking about prayer. The Meditation section is designed to facilitate a journey of getting to know God better, both in terms of how He sees us and how we see Him. It is the most important section of each session. Many people are unfamiliar with this kind of prayer and if so, the following suggestions about how to go about it should help with the start of the journey.

The aim is to enter the scene described in the passage and to see what develops. Before doing so, it helps to decide whether to be oneself or to imagine being one of the characters in the story and to choose which character. The members of the group need to be invited to do this and given time to decide who they are going to be. If meeting on zoom, it is a good idea to ask people to mute themselves before commencing. It is amazing how disruptive doorbells, incoming phone calls or other people in the house talking can be.

Next, it is helpful to 'dial down' to enable concentration. This can include inviting everyone to get comfortable, with feet on the floor and a straight back and then to relax, with eyes closed. One useful approach is to talk everyone through the different parts of the body, starting with the face and ending with the feet, tensing and then relaxing all the muscles. It is also helpful to become aware of one's breathing and to take a few deep breaths.

Then tell the group that you as leader will read an introduction to the scene, followed by the passage. The introductions offered at this point include a certain amount of imaginative conjecture at times, aimed at helping to get close to the scene and to those involved in it. Where there is basis for such conjecture, the sources are referenced in the Notes section at the back of the book. The passage is best read slowly, with gaps between each happening to allow people to imagine the scene unfolding. Unless the passage is a very long one, it is a good idea to read it twice and to let people know in advance how many times you will be reading it. At the end of reading the passage a time of silence of about five minutes is good, to allow the individuals taking part to complete what is happening for them. It is helpful if people know in advance to expect this. In order to determine when to bring the time of silence to a close, asking people to open their eyes when they have finished is a helpful way of gauging when people are ready.

Sharing what has been experienced in the scene can be important either by way of confession or in order to testify and make something more real. It is an opportunity to learn from each other and can also enable awareness of how to pray effectively for each other. Some people may find it too threatening and not want to share, others may be happy to share what comes up some weeks and not others. One way to handle this is to have an agreement that it is perfectly acceptable to say 'Pass' and not to share. Suggesting that people can do so makes it easy to ask anyone who hasn't shared yet whether they would like to do so without putting them under pressure or risking leaving them out inadvertently.

Sharing is best done in the form of one or two sentences which begin with: 'I was whichever character and I found myself' or 'I felt.' Some people, the author included, find this very difficult to do and may retell the story or notice things that are new to them at an intellectual level, rather than reporting their own responses to Jesus or the events surrounding Him. If this is welcomed, it can encourage such people to continue participating and through listening to those who are able to get in touch with their reactions and own them they can eventually learn to do the same.

Such sharing involves vulnerability and group boundaries will be needed to keep people safe. In the trial the group signed up to not repeating to anyone outside the group anything that was shared within the group and to not giving feedback to anyone's contribution, other than a thank you from the leader to acknowledge it. This might sound easy, but proved to be surprisingly difficult to maintain at times. If someone shares a sin that they have been challenged about, it can feel uncomfortable and the temptation to fix it can be strong. It is important to resist trying to make it alright for a number of reasons. Firstly, it will communicate to the person who said it that what they have said is not alright, which will risk them feeling rejected rather than forgiven. Secondly, if fixing the issue were easy they would not still be struggling with it, so to suggest solutions could feel simplistic and like a put down to the person on the receiving end and it will be unlikely that they will feel safe to share again going forward. Such responses are most likely if we are needing to distance ourselves from our own pain or sin, but will have the effect of alienating the person who has shared. Learning to listen in solidarity is a journey in itself. It challenges us to be open to our own pain and sinfulness as well as to other people's pain and to sit level with them in all our brokenness. If the leader finds this difficult, one safeguard is to invite the group to challenge them if they fall foul of the safety boundaries, just as they will do if any group member does. This should be explained to the group before any meditation is embarked upon.

Keeping a record of one's own discoveries during the meditations is a helpful way of remembering what might need to be processed with God on one's own or with a spiritual mentor at a later date, outside of the group. It is a good idea to suggest this to people and to encourage them to maintain their own journals.

OBSERVATIONS

The Observation sections were not part of the original script. Having translated the passage, written the comments and devised a list of questions for thought or discussion, the author was repeatedly surprised by the fact that yet more came out of the meditations, either at the time or during subsequent reflection following the end of the group session. Including her own observations is by way of encouragement that the meditations are worth doing and as an example of the kind of insights that one might expect to emerge. Most of the author's observations were reported to the group at the time, and they have been repeated in the first person, as shared with the group. It never ceased to be a source of surprise how different each person's experience of the meditation was week by week, sometimes because each person in the group chose to be a different character and often reflecting the fact that people in the group were at different places in their relationships with God. However, in line with the confidentiality agreement that the group had, no other contributions have been recorded, only the author's own. Because they are personal, they are best read after the meditation has been concluded, not beforehand. On a few occasions when completely unable to engage

INTRODUCTION

with the meditation the result was no observations and this has been recorded as 'Pass.' It is hoped that this will reinforce that it is perfectly acceptable for group members to decline to share their observations.

IN SUMMARY

The author has heard many sermons focussing on the stories that Jesus told, including the Sower, the Prodigal Son, the Wicked Steward and the Pearl of Great Price, to name but a few. She has never heard any sermons on the dynamics playing out between Jesus and those around Him, for example the interactions between Jesus and His disciples when they came to Him away from the crowds to ask questions about the meaning of His stories. It is Jesus' relationship dynamics that are the focus of the studies presented here. It is the author's prayer that these sessions will lead many into a deeper appreciation of what God is like and into a deeper relationship with Him.

PART 1

JESUS AND FATHER GOD

1

JESUS' BAPTISM

CONTEXT
Jesus grew up and worked in His father's business as a carpenter, based in a small and little-known village, Nazareth in Galilee, about sixteen miles from the Sea of Galilee.[1] We can conjecture that He would have been a skilled craftsman, producing items for people's homes and for their agricultural work.[2] These may well have included chests and tables, axe handles, and the yoke and shafts needed for harnessing oxen to a plough. He must have worked that way for over twenty years, by which time many of the farmers in the surrounding area would have owned, among other items, at least one yoke that He had made. Then, in His

early thirties, Jesus left His family and the business for an itinerant ministry. Before beginning His ministry, He walked the sixty or so miles from Galilee, parallel with the Jordan Valley, to a point not far north of the Dead Sea, where His relative, John the Baptist, was baptizing people in the River Jordan. There Jesus presented Himself to John for baptism.

John was about six months older than Jesus, the only son of an elderly priest called Zechariah, which means God remembers. Although the focus of Part One is on Jesus' human relationship with the Father, it is also worth considering the interactions of Zechariah, Mary and John with Father God, into which we are given brief insights and which were critical leading up to the event of Jesus' baptism. As John spent the whole of his adult life living in the wilderness, it is quite possible that John and Jesus had not met one another since attending festivals in Jerusalem as teenagers.

It would appear that Jesus' family may not have understood His apparent audacity in deserting His dependent mother and their source of livelihood. Certainly His neighbours from Nazareth did not understand. Jesus returned to Nazareth only briefly, and then moved either to Capernaum, where His cousins James and John lived, or possibly Bethsaida initially, whence Peter, Andrew and Philip came,[3] which might indicate that He was no longer welcome in the family home, or that He had to leave Nazareth before they could (Luke 4:16-30). We do not know for sure, what we do know is that Jesus later said of Himself that the Son of Man had nowhere to lay His head, implying that at some point in His life He experienced homelessness. Either way, in Galilee, Jesus and His followers would have been out of reach of Herod Antipas following the arrest of John the Baptist.[4]

JESUS' BAPTISM

MATTHEW 3:13-17

QUESTIONS FOR THOUGHT OR DISCUSSION

Who was John the Baptist? (Luke 1:36)

What answers to prayer were involved in the lead up to Jesus' baptism? (Luke 1:13-17, 24-25, 34-35, 38, Luke 3:2-3)

What did the prayers of Zechariah, Mary and John entail on their parts?

What had John's father prophesied over him when he was born? (Luke 1:76-79)

Why did the Jewish leaders send a delegation to ask John who he was and by what right he was baptizing? (John 1:19-28)

How did John describe himself? (John 1:23 and Isaiah 40:3)

How did John describe his ministry? (Luke 3:16)

What risks was John taking? (John 3:24)

What was the purpose of John's preaching and baptism? (John 1:31 and 3:28)

Whose authority did John have? (John 1:33)

What had God told John that would enable him to recognize who the Messiah was? (John 1:32-34)

Why do you think Jesus insisted on being baptized? (Matthew 3:15)

What did it cost Jesus to be baptized?

How did Father God respond immediately after Jesus was baptized? (Matthew 3:16-17)

COMMENTS

The Jews had been waiting a long time for their promised Messiah to appear. Four hundred years had elapsed since the last of the prophets, Malachi, had predicted that Elijah would return and now, at long last, there was a prophet out in the Judean wilderness, wearing a leather belt, just as Elijah had done. His appearance was timed to perfection, following a miraculous answer to the prayers of Zechariah and Elizabeth, that they might have a child in their old age. Zechariah's initial unbelief had been overridden and John the Baptist was born six months before Jesus. Mary's prayer, on being told by an angel that she would be giving birth to a son prior to marriage was one of query and submission, regardless of the possible consequences for herself. John the Baptist was also submitted and obedient to God.

When John started proclaiming that the Kingdom of Heaven was at hand and exhorting people to prepare the way of the Lord, it attracted attention. Word got around and people started flocking out into the wilderness, in order to be baptized in readiness. John had been promised by the Father that he would see the Holy Spirit resting on the One who would baptize with the Spirit, the Son of God, for whom he was preparing the way. We read in John's Gospel that John the Baptist saw this happening to Jesus as He approached him. On account of it, John resisted baptizing Jesus, stating that he needed to be baptized by Him, not the other way around. He was right of course, but Jesus resisted the temptation to concur with John. For Jesus, through whom the universe was created, to ask a creature who was part of that creation to baptize Him was a staggering gesture of humility. On top of which, Jesus had no sin from which He needed to repent. Nevertheless, He insisted that it was necessary to fulfil His Father's wishes and John baptized Him. Baptism was not only a turning from sin, first and foremost it signified a turning towards God. Jesus was identifying with human beings and pointing the way back to God. He was also marking a break from his previous life of working as a carpenter in the family business. Now, in obedience to the Father, He was making Himself available for full time ministry. The result was the anointing of the Holy Spirit, given to enable Jesus to fulfil what the Father was asking of Him. The Spirit appeared as a dove, possibly not an actual dove, but an impression of a spiritual reality of a kind that is normally invisible in the natural world. It was also a moment of ratification by the Father, by way of a voice from heaven announcing: "This is my beloved Son, and I am fully pleased with him." (NLT) The tense in the Greek is past: 'I was well pleased' implying 'in whom I was already well pleased,' which could be construed as indicating that Jesus had indeed had nothing from which He needed to repent.

MEDITATION
The track south from Galilee to Judea is through hot, dusty wilderness and miles of it. Every now and again there is a village, where food can be bought and where a well provides some drinking water. Some nights there is an Inn, other nights are spent in the open, sleeping round a fire for protection from the cold and from wild animals. There is plenty of time to think, several days and nights in fact. A time for adjustment on Jesus' part, or to wonder about the significance of Jesus' sudden change of direction. Once publicly baptized, there will be no going back. Then at last a crowd on the banks of the Jordan comes into view, just visible in the distance. There is a large, flat rock protruding out into the river and John is standing waist deep in the water.

> [13] Then Jesus came from Galilee to the Jordan to John, to be baptized by him. [14] But John would have hindered him, saying, "I need to be baptized by you, and you come to me?"

¹⁵ But Jesus, answering, said to him, "Allow it now, for this is the fitting way for us to fulfill all righteousness." Then he allowed him.

¹⁶ Jesus, when he was baptized, went up directly from the water: and behold, the heavens were opened to him. He saw the Spirit of God descending as a dove, and coming on him. ¹⁷ Behold, a voice out of the heavens said, "This is my beloved Son, with whom I am well pleased."

OBSERVATIONS

John's resistance to baptizing Jesus must have presented Jesus with the temptation to pull rank over John and not be baptized. The level of humility required on the part of Jesus, to allow a creature to baptize Him, when He was in fact the Word and Creator of the universe, is beyond imagining. He must have repeatedly faced temptations not to humble Himself, not to identify with us as a human being Himself and to reveal who He really was, Lord of creation. Jesus did not succumb to John's resistance. He steadfastly remained true to the call laid upon Him to identify Himself completely with what it means to be human and to exercise the humility required to do so. He was utterly focussed on pleasing the Father and responded to John accordingly.

Jesus' humility brought joy to the Father's heart.

2

"I THANK YOU, FATHER, LORD OF HEAVEN AND EARTH"

CONTEXT

Jesus had been instructing His disciples in preparation for sending them out in pairs to preach, heal and cast out demons without Him there. Having sent them on their way, He then set out Himself to teach and preach in one city after another, drawing crowds as He went. During His travels, He received a message from John the Baptist, by then in prison, appearing to question whether He really was the Messiah. Jesus responded by referring to the miracles that John's messengers had seen Him do, using familiar words from the prophet Isaiah that John would have recognized as a prediction of the Messiah. When John's messengers had left, Jesus began to bewail the lack of response to John's preaching and to castigate Chorazin, Bethsaida and Capernaum for their lack of repentance in response to Jesus' own miracles. He was talking to the crowds, very likely prior to the return of the disciples.

MATTHEW 11:20-30

QUESTIONS FOR THOUGHT OR DISCUSSION

What is the common expectation for the result of a mission today?

On what basis are missions commonly judged to have succeeded or failed?

If a mission is judged to have failed, what kind of soul searching goes on?

In what ways, if any, were Jesus' responses to the unbelief of people in His local towns different from our common responses to the outcome of a mission?

What was hidden from those who thought themselves wise and clever?

What did Jesus see as cause for thanksgiving to the Father?

What is the main characteristic of childlike people?

How do childlike people know anything?

What does Jesus' statement in verse 27 imply?

What was involved in 'coming to Jesus'?

"I THANK YOU, FATHER, LORD OF HEAVEN AND EARTH"

COMMENTS

In spite of Jesus' pain at the refusal of people living in His area to turn back to God, His approach to the Father was not at all downbeat. Somewhat surprisingly, here we find Jesus exclaiming His thanks to the Father for hiding the truth from the wise and clever and revealing it to babes. This raises the questions 'what truth?' and 'why would Jesus be pleased that it was hidden from anyone?' If we look further, we find that everything that Jesus knew was through revelation from the Father. The focus was not so much on the fact that anyone was excluded from knowing, as that Jesus was thanking the Father for His revelation and that in the light of it, we humans are not left to work it out for ourselves. If we try and do that, we will miss it. If we will admit that we cannot succeed in working it out and ask for revelation, we will receive it. That requires childlike humility, without which it is impossible to position ourselves rightly before God anyway, given who He is. Jesus was sharing His delight in the Father with Him. As a human being, even Jesus was dependent on the Father for what He knew, which is staggering in its humility, given who He was.

Jesus' next comment would also have appeared surprising to His listeners: "No one knows the Son, except the Father." Lots of people knew Jesus by this time and yet He was saying that none of them really knew Him. It is likely that He was talking about the fact that they saw Him as just another human being like them, when in fact He was far more than that. When Peter did finally realize that Jesus was the Messiah, Jesus immediately put Peter's realization down to the Father's revelation to him, in an interesting twist. Then, the Father was revealing Jesus' identity to Peter, here Jesus is saying that He Himself alone, knew the Father and was here to reveal the Father to others, but only those of His choosing. Both Father God and Jesus were focussed on making the other known. In proclaiming that no-one truly knew the Father except the Son, Jesus was setting Himself well and truly apart from the rest of humanity and claiming exceptional intimacy with the Father. The truth that was hidden from so many people was the truth of who He was and was only available through revelation, not by working it out using human reasoning.

This might sound as though Jesus was happy not to reveal who He was to everyone. However, His next statement negates that, as He invited all those listening and feeling weighed down to come to Him, for His yoke was easy. Anyone who owned a yoke that Jesus had crafted in His days as a carpenter would from then on have been reminded of Jesus' invitation to 'Come to Him,' each time they yoked their oxen to 'His' yoke.

Then Jesus made an astonishing claim, that He could give them rest. From the perspective of the Jewish leaders, Jesus was an untrained, upstart Rabbi. Yet in calling people to come to Himself it is hard not to hear a subtext behind what Jesus was saying, that people should come to Him and not to the established leaders of Israel. It is tempting to interpret Jesus' comments about being heavy laden as referring to life events in contemporary society. The words for 'labour and heavy laden' however can be translated as 'toiling and having been burdened.' Seen in context, this speaks of the burdens that the Pharisees were in the habit of laying on people. The covenant that the Jewish people had with God required them to keep God's law, but the Pharisees had embellished it with rules and regulations that were impossible to keep and that put untold pressure on people. All that people could hope for was to toil and still fail to come up to the mark. Pleasing God was impossible under such a system. Jesus was offering a let out. He had experienced the Father's pleasure in Him and He had just demonstrated His own gratitude to the Father. Now He invited others to join this fellowship of mutual love and appreciation. To those who came to Him, He extended love and acceptance, forgiveness, healing and graciousness. If they would learn from Him, they would find that what He asked of them was easier for them than the load laid on them by the Pharisees and Sadducees.

Gentleness and lowliness were characteristics that Jesus both claimed for Himself and demonstrated. He would sit level, or even beneath other people and take care not to ride roughshod over them. Being a disciple is challenging, it involves carrying our cross; but eventually those who come to Jesus and follow Him will realize that having an assurance of acceptance by God and resurrection to eternal life provides a context of love and security.

MEDITATION
You have heard that Jesus is in the area, and you are setting out to find Him. You have been hearing a lot about Him recently and you are intrigued to understand why everyone is talking about Him so much. Your neighbour, who is extremely sceptical about the reports of Jesus, decides to join you out of curiosity. You are in luck, as you have caught up with Jesus in time to witness Him talking to John the Baptist's disciples. They have delivered John's question about who Jesus is and you hear first-hand Jesus telling them that He has been healing the blind and lame, curing lepers, restoring hearing to the deaf and raising dead people. You recognize that it is what was predicted of the Messiah in Isaiah 61. You hear Him telling John's disciples to repeat what they have seen to John. You see John's followers set off to take Jesus' message back to John, and wonder what will become of John. Jesus brings you out of your reverie with a start, as He is reinforcing His message about who He is by describing John as the messenger sent to prepare the way for Him, this time referring to Malachi 3. Can Jesus really be the Messiah, for whom you have been waiting for so long? He seems to think that of Himself. And He is doing all the things predicted of the Messiah. This is momentous. By now you have followed Him up a hill overlooking the Sea of Galilee, where it is easier to hear what He is saying from a distance. You are trying to keep as near to the front of the crowd as you can, but there are a lot of other people wanting to do the same, so it isn't easy. And now Jesus is castigating your hometown of Bethsaida. This isn't what you expected to hear when you set out! And then quite seamlessly and unexpectedly He moves from talking to you to addressing Yahweh, as though He knew Him intimately. You have never heard the leader of your synagogue pray this way ever. It isn't even allowed to say God's name and yet Jesus is calling Him Daddy. This is a lot to get your head around.

[20] Then he began to denounce the cities in which most of his mighty works had been done, because they didn't repent. [21] "Woe to you, Chorazin! Woe to you, Bethsaida! For if the mighty works had been done in Tyre and Sidon which were done in you, they would have repented long ago in sackcloth and ashes. [22] But I tell you, it will be more tolerable for Tyre and Sidon on the day of judgment than for you. [23] You, Capernaum, who are exalted to heaven, you will go down to Hades. For if the mighty works had been done in Sodom which were done in you, it would have remained until today. [24] But I tell you that it will be more tolerable for the land of Sodom on the day of judgment, than for you."

[25] At that time, Jesus answered, "I thank you, Father, Lord of heaven and earth, that you hid these things from the wise and understanding, and revealed them to infants. [26] Yes, Father, for so it was well-pleasing in your sight. [27] All things have been delivered to me by my Father. No one knows the Son, except the Father; neither does anyone know the Father, except the Son and he to whom the Son desires to reveal him.

[28] "Come to me, all you who labor and are heavily burdened, and I will give you rest. [29] Take my yoke upon you and learn from me, for I am gentle and humble in heart; and you will find rest for your souls. [30] For my yoke is easy, and my burden is light."

OBSERVATIONS

The lack of repentance in response to Jesus' healing miracles in Capernaum and the other cities in the area must have hurt Him. What more did He need to do to win back the hearts of His beloved people? It was the kind of situation that gets analysed following a contemporary mission. If there hasn't been significant growth in numbers in the church as a result, it is tempting to pronounce the enterprise a failure. That can result in looking for reasons and either self-blame or disaffection with God for setting one up for rejection. Jesus did not go down either of those paths, rather He turned to the Father in His disappointment with thanksgiving and appreciation for who the Father is.

The sudden change from addressing the Father to talking about Him seemed rather disjointed, until I thought of it in terms of what I do when I write to God. When I have finished, I write 'Dear Jane' on the page and then listen and wait to see what comes into my mind. Seen in the light of that, verse 27 looks like the Father's answer to Jesus' prayer, which Jesus reports out loud in summary form, as part of the dialogue between Him and the Father. The Father knows exactly how Jesus feels about the rejection that He is experiencing; the Father feels it too. No-one else would even be able to imagine what it was like. When it came to revelation, Jesus had it one hundred per cent, in complete humility, again unlike anyone else. In the light of which Jesus, and only Jesus, was perfectly placed to reveal the Father to the people. Encouraged and strengthened by the solidarity of Father God and reminded of His unique position, Jesus immediately turned to the people and laid Himself open to the possibility of further rejection with an invitation that left people equally free to respond either positively or negatively. What amazing vulnerability and sustained by an equally amazing prayer life! What an insight into Jesus' honouring of the Father, regardless of how people were responding to Him. Followed by further insight into the Father's affirmation of and encouragement for Jesus. In the light of it, Jesus wasted no time in demonstrating that God's concern for His people's welfare and His desire to be known by them overrode any concerns that He might have had about His own safety or need to protect Himself from rejection.

Revelation brings with it responsibility. The Father wants to be known by His people, regardless of the risk of rejection and if we know Him, wants us to make Him known. Sharing in Father God's affirmation and encouragement, if we proclaim Him and suffer for it, is part of Jesus' legacy to us.

3

RAISING OF LAZARUS

CONTEXT

It was the middle of winter, time for the annual Jewish Festival of Dedication, otherwise known as Hanukkah or Festival of Lights, which often coincides with Christmas. The festival was a celebration of the rededication of the Temple in 164 BC, following the Maccabean revolt. The ruler Antiochus IV had tried to force the Jews to adopt Greek religion and in 167 BC had installed an altar to Zeus in the Temple and instructed that pigs should be sacrificed on it. Judah, nicknamed Maccabeus (meaning hammer), the son of a priest and Judah's men eventually gained control of Jerusalem, tore down the altar to Zeus and built a new one to Yahweh. They also relit the seven branched candlestick, or menorah. The one jar of undefiled oil that they found, which would normally only have lasted for one day, lasted for eight days, giving them time to prepare more oil to keep the menorah, which was never allowed to go out, alight.[5]

During the festival, Jesus stood in the Temple and proclaimed: "I am the good shepherd" (John 10:14). It was a Messianic reference to Ezekiel 34:11-12, which states that the word of the Lord came to Ezekiel telling him to prophesy against the shepherds of Israel for feeding themselves and not the sheep. In verse 15 we read: "'I myself will be the shepherd of my sheep, and I will cause them to lie down,' says the Lord Yahweh." This passage was part of the liturgy at the festival. The Jewish leaders responded by surrounding Jesus, demanding that He should tell them whether or not He really was the Messiah. Jesus replied saying that He had already told them, but they had not believed Him, because they were not of His flock. He then went on to say that His sheep would listen to His voice and He would give them eternal life, as His Father had given them to Him and He and the Father were one. The Jews were incensed that Jesus had made Himself God and took up stones to throw at Him and then tried to arrest Him, but Jesus escaped. Because His life was clearly in danger, Jesus withdrew from Jerusalem and went down into the Jordan Valley and across the Jordan River. He very likely passed through Bethany, two miles from Jerusalem and it would have been easy for him to tell Mary and Martha where He was going. Then He passed through Jericho, eighteen miles from Jerusalem, on His journey to the Jordan River. He stayed near the place where John the Baptist first baptized people and many people followed Him there. He was probably about forty miles from Jerusalem, a two or three-day journey on foot. While He was there, Mary and Martha sent Him a message, telling Him that their brother Lazarus was sick. He stayed where He was for two more days and then, despite the danger, set off for Bethany, accompanied by His disciples.

GOD'S HEART FOR ANSWERING PRAYER

JOHN 11:38-44

QUESTIONS FOR THOUGHT OR DISCUSSION

What might the implications of Jesus' delay in reaching Bethany have been?

What do Jesus' feelings tell us about how God views human suffering?

What did Jesus have in mind in telling those present to take away the stone that sealed the grave?

Do you think that having the stone removed was a difficult thing for Jesus to do?

What does Martha's reaction tell us about the level of her trust in Jesus?

Did Martha succeed in deterring Jesus from His intended course of action?

Did Jesus overrule Martha's right as next of kin to refuse the reopening of the tomb?

What had Jesus done previously that enabled Him to help Martha fall into line with His purposes at this point? (John 11:20-27)

What does Jesus' prayer indicate to us about His relationship with the Father?

Do you get the impression that Jesus already knew that the Father wanted Him to raise Lazarus from the dead?

What was Jesus' chief motivation for raising Lazarus from the dead?

Why was Jesus so keen for people to realize who He was?

How did people respond after seeing Lazarus coming out of the tomb alive?

COMMENTS

An obvious question is, 'why did Jesus wait for two days before He and the disciples set out for Bethany?' It is likely that they had to walk forty miles to get there, which amounted to a journey lasting two or three days. They arrived four days too late. Had they set out two days earlier, they would still have arrived two days too late. However, the Jews believed that a person's soul hovered over their body for three days following death, until the body started to change. Had Jesus arrived two days earlier than He did, not enough time would have elapsed for Lazarus' death to be confirmed beyond doubt. Two people were known to have been found alive in their tombs in the past and to have subsequently lived to old age, hence a Jewish custom of visiting the tomb to inspect the body during the three days following death.[6] Mary and Martha would have done this the day prior to Jesus' arrival. Jesus' delay ensured that the extra two days needed to check that the death was real had elapsed by the time He got there, so that no sceptic could claim that He had not in fact raised Lazarus from the dead. This may well explain why Jesus delayed going, under the Father's direction and why He had told His followers that He was glad not to have been there when Lazarus died, so that they might believe (John 11:15).

Jesus had clearly asked the Father for Lazarus' life to be saved and his death meanwhile has not deterred Jesus in any way. As a human being Jesus had no power over death, but the Father did and Jesus was leaning on Him now, completely. He had no doubts, rather absolute certainty, apparently based on 100% track record in answers to prayer. Nothing for which Jesus had ever asked had displeased the Father or been contrary to His will. Nothing had been outside of His power and ability. Never had Jesus doubted the Father's ability to deliver. There had been complete unanimity between them throughout. They were as one, with absolutely no communication barrier at any point.

Through what Jesus said, we see His desire that He might be known and recognized for who He was, that relationship with the individuals in the crowd might become possible between Himself and them and by implication between the Father and them. If they once recognized that Jesus had been sent by Father God, it would amount to a recognition that He was indeed the Messiah, the long awaited One, the Saviour promised through the prophets of old. Elijah and Elisha apart, no-one else had ever been able to raise the dead.

Many of the Jews who were visiting Mary and Martha put their faith in Jesus following this miracle. Others went and informed the Pharisees, for whom it was the last straw. They were afraid of Roman retaliation if the people went after an alternative God to Caesar and so they set out to silence Jesus once and for all.

MEDITATION

You are standing on the side of a hill, not far from the village of Bethany, on dry and dusty earth. Ahead are several caves, some open and others sealed with stones. You are not alone, there is quite a large crowd; Jesus, His disciples, Mary, Martha, their friends and relatives from Jerusalem and from Bethany. The atmosphere is heavy with grief. Everyone is distressed, some are weeping openly and others are silent. Nobody knows how Mary and Martha will survive now that they have lost their breadwinner and protector. No-one is talking.

> [38] Jesus therefore, again groaning in himself, came to the tomb. Now it was a cave, and a stone lay against it. [39] Jesus said, "Take away the stone."
>
> Martha, the sister of him who was dead, said to him, "Lord, by this

time there is a stench, for he has been dead four days."

⁴⁰ Jesus said to her, "Didn't I tell you that if you believed, you would see God's glory?"

⁴¹ So they took away the stone from the place where the dead man was lying. Jesus lifted up his eyes, and said, "Father, I thank you that you listened to me. ⁴² I know that you always listen to me, but because of the multitude standing around I said this, that they may believe that you sent me." ⁴³ When he had said this, he cried with a loud voice, "Lazarus, come out!"

⁴⁴ He who was dead came out, bound hand and foot with wrappings, and his face was wrapped around with a cloth.

Jesus said to them, "Free him, and let him go."

OBSERVATIONS

What was not to like about a guy who could raise the dead? Mary and Martha must have been overwhelmed with gratitude. We see the outpouring of it when Mary, not long afterwards, anointed Jesus with incredibly valuable perfume. Others who were present responded with belief in who He was, but not all. Some went scurrying back to Jerusalem to report to the Pharisees what Jesus had done now. Presumably they were regular worshippers at the Temple and known to the Pharisees. They must have known that the Pharisees would not be happy about the news. Maybe they were afraid that if they did not report it themselves, the Pharisees would suspect them of believing in Jesus and banish them from the congregation. This would have meant becoming ostracized by friends and family alike, and being treated little better than the lepers, a terrifying prospect.

The Pharisees, for their part, had mixed reasons for fearing Jesus. Jealousy that He was gaining a following, which meant that they were losing theirs, was undoubtedly part of it. It went much deeper than that though. As religious leaders in a religious state that was ruled by a foreign power, they were well aware of the need to placate Rome, in order to protect the Temple and the status quo. With Caesar and Jesus each claiming the right to people's allegiance on account of their divine status, there was, to the Pharisees' way of thinking, obvious danger in allowing the people to follow Jesus, and by implication, not Caesar. Their bottom-line allegiance to Caesar, as opposed to Yahweh, became apparent when they called for Jesus to be crucified, telling Pilate that he was no friend of Caesar's if he ignored their wishes. The irony was that they took themselves out of Yahweh's protection in the process and Rome sacked Jerusalem as a result.

Trusting (or fearing) the powers we can see, rather than the One we cannot see, won't end well, either for us or for the society in which we live. The One we cannot see is the ultimate Power, wanting to bring life, rather than death and destruction.

4

JESUS' PRAYER FOR HIS FOLLOWERS

CONTEXT

After having raised Lazarus from the dead and knowing that the Pharisees would not welcome the news, Jesus retreated with His disciples to a village called Ephraim, in the mountainous country north-east of Jerusalem, where He stayed for several weeks. Until, that is, it was time for the Passover Festival. That occasioned the return of Jesus and His disciples to Bethany and from there to Jerusalem. Many of the Jews had heard about Lazarus by that time and when Jesus entered Jerusalem riding on a donkey, the crowds laid palm branches in His path and chanted 'Hosanna,' (meaning, 'Save, we pray.') This indicated that many of the Jews had concluded that Jesus must be the Messiah, given that He had raised Lazarus from the dead.

Later that same week we read in great detail the course of the conversation between Jesus and His disciples at His last meal with them, on the Wednesday evening before He was crucified.[7] At the end of the conversation Jesus turned to prayer. We often read of Jesus praying to the Father with no indication of what He prayed being recorded for us. This time John witnessed the contents of Jesus' prayer and remembered and recorded it. It is the longest prayer of Jesus to which we have access and it is quite long!

JOHN 17:1-26

QUESTIONS FOR THOUGHT OR DISCUSSION

What did Jesus mean when He said, "Father, the time has come"?

Why did Jesus pray for the Father to bring glory to Him?

Would the crucifixion have seemed in any way like an answer to Jesus' prayer for glory to either Jesus or His disciples?

What was the authority that the Father had given to Jesus?

How did Jesus define eternal life?

What was Jesus' verdict on His own life?

What was Jesus' final prayer for Himself?

What had the disciples learned through being with Jesus?

How had the disciples responded to Jesus?

How might Jesus have felt about leaving the disciples to return to the Father?

What did Jesus ask the Father to do for His disciples?

What did Jesus pray for people who would hear the disciples' message?

COMMENTS

Jesus' immediate focus was on the Father's glory. It is reminiscent of His lesson on how to pray: "Our Father in heaven, may your name be honoured." (NLT) However, in order that the Father may be glorified, Jesus asked Him to glorify Jesus Himself. There is something very mutual going on here. Then the purpose of it all, the giving of eternal life to His followers, thus reversing the death sentence hanging over humanity since Adam and Eve rebelled against God. Then the crux of it all, that eternal life consisted in knowing the Father and recognizing that Jesus had been sent by Him. Knowing implies being one with.

Jesus then professed that He had indeed glorified the Father on earth through completing the work that the Father had given Him to do, with the result that the disciples had believed that Jesus had been sent by the Father. Jesus prayed that in His absence the Father would keep the disciples in the world and protect them from the evil one, that they would be set apart for Him in truth, know His joy and be one with the Father and with each other. This would amount to holiness and the ability to proclaim the coming of God's Kingdom on earth through Jesus. Jesus did not stop there, He prayed for all those who would believe in Him on hearing the disciples' message, that the world might believe that He had been sent by the Father and that He loved them, plus that the Father's love might be in them and that they might be one, as Jesus and the Father are one.

MEDITATION

Jesus and His disciples are together for the Last Supper and you are there with them. Jesus is acutely aware of the fact that it is indeed His last meal, but the disciples have not understood it yet. You are meeting in secret in a large upper room in Jerusalem, belonging to a friend of Jesus. You are aware that being there is putting all your lives in danger. There are no servants present, so Jesus has washed everyone's feet Himself. There is a large table in the middle of the room and all the men present are reclining around it. There was a lot of food on the table earlier on, which has now been eaten. Judas has left to betray Jesus to the religious rulers, but none of you but Jesus has understood why Judas has suddenly departed. There is still so much that Jesus wants you all to know. That He is going to leave you, that you should love one another, that you can ask anything of the Father in Jesus' name, and you will receive what you ask for, that He, Jesus, is the true vine, and that you should remain in Him, that you will be persecuted, that Jesus has come from the Father and is going back to Him. It is a lot to take in!

Then, as if all that is not enough, Jesus turns His eyes upwards and addresses the Father in your hearing.

> 17 Jesus said these things, then lifting up his eyes to heaven, he said, "Father, the time has come. Glorify your Son, that your Son may also glorify you; ² even as you gave him authority over all flesh, so he will give eternal life to all whom you have given him. ³ This is eternal life, that they should know you, the only true God, and him whom you sent, Jesus Christ. ⁴ I glorified you on the earth. I have accomplished the work which you have given me to do. ⁵ Now, Father, glorify me with your own self with the glory which I had with you before the world existed. ⁶ I revealed your name to the people whom you have given me out of the world. They were yours, and you have given them to me. They have kept your word. ⁷ Now they have known that all things whatever you have given me are from you, ⁸ for the words which you have given me I have given to them, and they received

them, and knew for sure that I came from you. They have believed that you sent me. ⁹ I pray for them. I don't pray for the world, but for those whom you have given me, for they are yours. ¹⁰ All things that are mine are yours, and yours are mine, and I am glorified in them. ¹¹ I am no more in the world, but these are in the world, and I am coming to you. Holy Father, keep them through your name which you have given me, that they may be one, even as we are. ¹² While I was with them in the world, I kept them in your name. I have kept those whom you have given me. None of them is lost except the son of destruction, that the Scripture might be fulfilled. ¹³ But now I come to you, and I say these things in the world, that they may have my joy made full in themselves. ¹⁴ I have given them your word. The world hated them, because they are not of the world, even as I am not of the world. ¹⁵ I pray not that you would take them from the world, but that you would keep them from the evil one. ¹⁶ They are not of the world even as I am not of the world. ¹⁷ Sanctify them in your truth. Your word is truth. <u>Psalm 119:142</u> ¹⁸ As you sent me into the world, even so I have sent them into the world. ¹⁹ For their sakes I sanctify myself, that they themselves also might be sanctified in truth. ²⁰ Not for these only do I pray, but for those also who will believe in me through their word, ²¹ that they may all be one; even as you, Father, are in me, and I in you, that they also may be one in us; that the world may believe that you sent me. ²² The glory which you have given me, I have given them; that they may be one, even as we are one; ²³ I in them, and you in me, that they may be perfected into one; that the world may know that you sent me and loved them, even as you loved me. ²⁴ Father, I desire that they also whom you have given me be with me where I am, that they may see my glory, which you have given me, for you loved me before the foundation of the world. ²⁵ Righteous Father, the world hasn't known you, but I knew you; and these knew that you sent me. ²⁶ I made known to them your name, and will make it known; that the love with which you loved me may be in them, and I in them."

OBSERVATIONS

Jesus perfectly reflects the Father's heart in the way that He prays. There is immense care and concern for the well-being of His followers, that they be protected from the evil one, that they would know joy, that they would be pure and holy and entirely the Father's even while remaining in the world, that they would be one, that they would see the Father's glory and reflect it to the world, that they would continue to receive revelation of the Father from Jesus and that they would know His love within them and Jesus dwelling within them. There is a strong sense of Jesus' awareness that the Father would be watching over His own, both at the time of Jesus' crucifixion and throughout the future yet to come. Jesus has discharged the responsibility given to Him by the Father to keep His followers safe and now He hands responsibility back to the Father, with total trust and confidence. His followers and the future are secure in the Father's hands. This was Jesus' prayer and the Father's heart for every one of His followers, including those of us alive today.

5

JESUS IN GETHSEMANE

CONTEXT

The Jews had been led to expect a Messiah to appear and had been waiting for a long time. It was four hundred years since they had even had a prophet, the most recent one was Malachi. Having been over-run by the Romans and become a vassal state, they had become familiar with Roman troops being in evidence to maintain peace. Jesus created a stir by making repeated Messianic claims, which were obvious to anyone who knew their Hebrew Scriptures. The Jewish authorities were jealous of Jesus' following, which arose on account of the many healings and miracles that He performed. The authorities were also afraid of the

Romans and of the fact that Jesus' Messianic claims were in direct conflict with Caesar's claim to ultimate allegiance. The authorities feared Caesar sacking Jerusalem and demolishing the Temple, which the Romans had the power and military might to do. The Jewish leaders therefore decided that they needed to silence Jesus and they were intent on arresting Him, but without creating unrest on the part of the people. Jesus was aware of His impending betrayal and death.

MATTHEW 26:36-46

QUESTIONS FOR THOUGHT OR DISCUSSION

What, if anything, do you know about Gethsemane?

To whom did Jesus turn in His distress?

What did Jesus ask of those to whom He had turned in His distress?

Did Jesus receive what He was hoping for from His companions? Or from Father God?

What was involved for Jesus in saying 'Yes' to the Father's will?

What enabled Jesus to say 'Yes'? (Matthew 20:17-19, Hebrews 12:2)

In what ways does Jesus' prayer reflect His teaching earlier in the Gospel story? (Matthew 6:10, Matthew 22:36-40)

What does Jesus' prayer tell us about what it means to love the Lord with all our heart, mind, soul and strength?

What answer to His prayer in Gethsemane did Jesus receive from the Father?

What does Jesus' experience of prayer in Gethsemane tell us about the Father's heart for answering prayer?

COMMENTS

Gethsemane means press of olives. It is likely that it was the site of a private olive press, situated in a cave in which there would have been a constant temperature conducive to the process of pressing olives. Nowhere in the Gospels are we told this, but nor are we told that it was a garden, although this has commonly been envisaged since. However, as early as the fourth century a pilgrim called Egeria wrote in her diary that the location of Gethsemane was a revered cave.[8] What we can surmise is that it was a place in which Jesus and His disciples were accustomed to spending time, maybe because they were unable to afford the price of accommodation inside Jerusalem at festival time. There would have been many other people staying on the Mount of Olives in the week leading up to the Passover, so it would appear that it was somewhere private, to which they could retreat sure of access in the middle of the night, suggesting that one of them had a key. One thing we can be sure of and that is that Judas knew where to find them.

Arriving at Gethsemane, Jesus was looking into an abyss. Total nothingness. His body was going to be slain. He had to give up everything. Death was staring Him in the face, and it was terrifying. He asked the disciples closest to Him for support as He retreated further into the cave to pray.

"Daddy, if possible, no! Yet not as I wish, but as You wish."

Who would look after His mother now? His brothers didn't believe in Him, they would not offer any comfort. How would she manage without Him?

"Daddy, as You wish."

He had so much life still ahead of Him, so much teaching He could still do, so many who still had not recognized Him.

"Daddy, as You wish."

He would not be around to see how His nieces and nephews developed. What would happen to them when the Romans came to sack the Temple?

"Daddy, as You wish."

The Jewish leaders were going to declare Him worthy of death, for doing nothing worse than being Himself and letting His identity be known.

"Daddy, if this cannot be taken away but I drink it, let Your will be done."

Pilate will condemn Him to death for no better reason than to avert a riot and save his own skin.

"Daddy, if this cannot be taken away but I drink it, let Your will be done."

500 Roman soldiers will mock Him, scourge Him, spit on Him, deride Him.

"Daddy, Your will, not Mine."

The Jewish leaders will taunt Him, "He saved others, let him save himself if he is really God's Chosen One, the Messiah." (NLT) The criminal beside Him will do the same.

"Daddy, let Your will be done."

Worst of all by far, the absolute oneness between Him and Daddy will be severed.

"Daddy, let Your will be done."

Jesus' utter passion for the Father and the Father's will overrode every reason He had for wanting to avoid suffering crucifixion. Even this unimaginable prospect could not destroy their one-ness and integrity as God. Jesus overcame every temptation He faced and submitted His will to His Father out of His love for Him. He had absolutely no self-interest.

MEDITATION
You have spent a couple of hours celebrating a Passover meal late at night with Jesus and His other closest friends and Jesus has been teaching at length, as though there were no tomorrow. Upstairs and behind locked doors, you have feared interruption by the Jewish authorities, wanting to arrest Jesus. You could not stay the night there, so you are transferring to a cave called Gethsemane on the Mount of Olives, a place you all know well, having spent other nights there in the past. The moon is almost full, which helps you to see where you are going as you make your way around the outside of the city walls along the Kidron Valley in the middle of the night.[9] You feel quite a conspicuous crowd so you walk in complete silence and without torches. It is a relief to finally arrive at the Mount of Olives and the cave where you expect to spend the night. There are many other pilgrims camping out for the night ready for the festival, some of them huddled around fires, as there is not enough accommodation in Jerusalem to go round. You just want to lie down and go to sleep, but Jesus has other ideas. He wants to pray and He wants support. You attempt to stay awake at His request.

³⁶ Then Jesus came with them to a place called Gethsemane, and said to his disciples, "Sit here, while I go there and pray." ³⁷ He took with him Peter and the two sons of Zebedee, and began to be sorrowful and severely troubled. ³⁸ Then he said to them, "My soul is exceedingly sorrowful, even to death. Stay here and watch with me."

³⁹ He went forward a little, fell on his face, and prayed, saying, "My Father, if it is possible, let this cup pass away from me; nevertheless, not what I desire, but what you desire."

⁴⁰ He came to the disciples and found them sleeping, and said to Peter, "What, couldn't you watch with me for one hour? ⁴¹ Watch and pray, that you don't enter into temptation. The spirit indeed is willing, but the flesh is weak."

⁴² Again a second time he went away and prayed, saying, "My Father, if this cup can't pass away from me unless I drink it, your desire be done."

⁴³ He came again and found them sleeping, for their eyes were heavy. ⁴⁴ He left them again, went away, and prayed a third time, saying the same words. ⁴⁵ Then he came to his disciples and said to them, "Are you still sleeping and resting? Behold, the hour is at hand, and the Son of Man is betrayed into the hands of sinners. ⁴⁶ Arise, let's be going. Behold, he who betrays me is at hand."

OBSERVATIONS

The trust and security between Jesus and the Father was ultimate. Jesus felt totally at liberty to tell the Father exactly how He felt, even when He wanted a let out from their long-term plan for the salvation of the world. The Father, for His part, remained silent and appeared not to respond to Jesus' request for a let-out, in spite of the pain that it must have cost Him. The Father was focussed on His commitment to re-opening the door to His presence for humanity and was willing to take the pain involved. The price of God's love for us is unimaginable. When the Father ignored Jesus' request, Jesus submitted to His side of the pain for love of the Father.

While the disciples slept, Jesus was battling to maintain an unsullied focus on His Father and the Father's will. In the process He was letting go of all His attachments to this world and His concerns for the welfare of His family. More fundamentally, He was also overcoming His fear of death and separation from the Father's presence. Everything needed to be placed in the Father's hands in total trust. He was winning the battle against temptation to act out of self-interest in secret, so that He would be able to go through with the Father's will in public. The disciples, meanwhile, were doing no such thing and subsequently fell into temptation and deserted Jesus to different degrees, on account of their fear.

6

DEATH OF JESUS

CONTEXT
Following His arrest, Jesus was kept up for the rest of the night. Initially He was taken before Caiaphas, the high priest. (Caiaphas was the one who had declared to the Sanhedrin, after Jesus raised Lazarus from the dead, that it would be better for one man to die for the people, than for all to die. Ever since then the Jewish leaders had been intent on arresting Jesus and having Him put to death). The following morning, the Jewish leaders conducted a mock trial, looking for two witnesses to agree on something of which they could accuse Jesus. They found none who could agree on anything sufficiently substantial to persuade the Romans that Jesus was

worthy of death. In the end they decided to go for blasphemy charges, in response to Jesus' own words. They knew that that would mean nothing to Pilate, but they sent Jesus to him anyway, as they did not have the power to condemn anyone to death, only the Romans could do that. The Jewish leaders' accusation was that Jesus had claimed to be the King of the Jews. They well knew that that was political dynamite.

Pilate tried hard to release Jesus. However, the Jews requested the release of an alternative prisoner and that Jesus should be crucified. When Pilate objected, they accused him of being no friend of Caesar's. Pilate was more frightened by that than he was by a message from his wife telling of a dream and warning him to have nothing to do with Jesus. He caved in to the Jewish leaders, while at the same time attempting to disclaim responsibility.

Having condemned Jesus to death within hours of His arrest, Pilate had a sign written, declaring "This is the King of the Jews." (NLT) Jesus was mocked and scourged by the soldiers and then led out of the Praetorium to be crucified. An African guy from Cyrene called Simon was co-opted by the Romans to carry the cross for Jesus.

On reaching Golgotha (meaning the Place of the Skull), the Roman soldiers nailed Jesus to the cross and hauled it into place. The chief priests, passers-by and criminals either side of Him all hurled insults at Him, taunting Him to prove His identity by coming down from the cross.

MATTHEW 27:45-56

QUESTIONS FOR THOUGHT OR DISCUSSION

What do you think might have caused the darkness surrounding Jesus' death?

What temptations did Jesus face while hanging on the cross? (Matthew 26:53-54, 27:41-44)

Jesus appears to have known His destiny, so why did He feel abandoned?

How must it have felt for Jesus, not to see God's vindication of Him?

Do you see a connection between what was happening on the cross and the events in the natural world?

Do you see the strange events as communication from Father God?

If so, with whom was Father God communicating?

What did the darkness and earthquake signify?

What did the Roman centurion conclude from the darkness and earthquake?

What does Father God's apparent silence while Jesus was dying tell us about Father God's heart for answering prayer?

COMMENTS

It was lunchtime on a sunny day in August. The author was in St Ives, looking out over the harbour from a good vantage point, surrounded by a loose crowd of people doing the same thing. Slowly, almost imperceptibly, the daylight began to fade. The boatmen collected their boats into lines and moored them outside the harbour, as the tide was going out. The streetlights came on along the Wharf. The seagulls started squawking, as though preparing to turn in for the night. Gradually it got darker, and then darker, and then darker still, until nothing was visible except for the streetlights and the stars. The harbour and the boats outside it disappeared from view and the seagulls became silent. Nothing moved, everything was silent, eerily silent. It was far too early for the sun to set. But its light was gone and with it, its warmth. Suddenly it became deathly cold. What would happen if the sun failed to reappear, I wondered? The cold was getting worse, and it was too dark to move about safely. For how much longer would it last? I thought how terrifying it must have been for ancient peoples to experience such an event, not knowing what was happening, nor for how long it would last. I, of course, knew that the moon was passing in front of the sun and that it would take all of eight minutes before normality was gradually restored. Even so I felt as though the world had gone out of control and that I was powerless to put it right. I felt so vulnerable, so much more aware of my dependency on the natural world than previously. It was normally so dependable and so easy to take it for granted. That casual certainty was gone forever.

It was lunchtime on an ancient day in spring. Jesus was hanging on a cross. The whole land became dark and remained that way for three hours. There would have been no remote-controlled streetlights then, only torches or a fire, hastily got together maybe. Or maybe not. It must have been bitterly cold long before three o'clock. Jesus and the criminals either side of Him would have been freezing by that time. Impossible for them to see who was left in the crowd, if anyone. Impossible for the crowd to watch the indignity to which Jesus and the criminals were being subjected. For the Roman soldiers, keeping guard, it must have seemed as though the sun would never return, and the world was coming to an abrupt and unexpected end. Completely terrifying.

It needs saying that the analogy with a solar eclipse has limits to its value. The darkness surrounding Jesus' death lasted too long for it to be explained in terms of an eclipse. It is more likely that the darkness was caused by a sandstorm, common in the middle east at the time of year when Jesus died.[10] However, the loss of the sun's light and heat and uncertainty about the duration would all have been present in either event.

At about three o'clock Jesus cried out with a loud voice. How could He still breathe after six hours of hanging there? The Greek word for cried has a prefix which denotes upwards. He cried upwards, "My God, my God, why have you forsaken me?" Gone is the normally familiar way that Jesus addressed the Father when He was talking to Him within earshot of others. Father is better translated Daddy; He was normally so intimate with Him. But that has changed. The Father now seems distant and aloof. Jesus appears to have lost His certainty about always being heard. It seems that God is no longer one. For God to be alienated within Himself when His very nature is love defies imagination. Or maybe Jesus quoted Psalm 22 in order to emphasize its prophetic content and the fact that it was right then being fulfilled. Either way, Jesus had set His face toward Jerusalem, He had tried to prepare His disciples, so that they would not lose their faith, but now it seems that nothing could have prepared Him for what the cross entailed. He was dying abandoned, alienated from the Father and in freezing, pitch black agony. Heaven remained silent throughout.

Until the moment after Jesus had died, that is. Then the darkness retreated, and the Roman soldiers were exposed to yet another source of terror; the ground beneath them was shaking and the rocks were splitting apart. "Please not the rocks on which we stand." It might have seemed to Jesus that God was silent throughout the crucifixion, but the Romans present were able to understand the message of the darkness and the earthquake only too well. The centurion and the others who were with him concluded that Jesus truly was the Son of God. A complete turnaround in attitude from the mocking way that they had treated Him only hours before. The curtain in the Temple being rent in two might have passed them by, but the Jews would have been given pause for thought by that and by the appearance of some of their dead relatives a couple of days later. God might not have vindicated Jesus while He was being treated as a quack and taunted with questions designed to tempt Him to prove His identity by skipping death, but the Father wasted no time in communicating the significance of the event the moment it was over.

MEDITATION

You are horrified by what is happening to Jesus. He has been arrested and is on trial before Pilate inside the Praetorium. In spite of your fear for yourself as a known follower of Jesus, you need to know what is going to happen next. You do not want to be at the mercy of conflicting, second hand reports after the event, when it will be too late to find out what really happened. So you hang around outside the Praetorium until Jesus emerges, and Simon is co-opted to carry a cross for Him. Now you know what is coming next and your worst fears are being realized. You follow along in the crowd, feeling utterly powerless to do anything to help Jesus. You see the soldiers and Jesus reaching Golgotha, one of the Romans' favourite crucifixion sites, just outside the walls of Jerusalem. You cannot bear to watch, but nor can you bring yourself to leave. You hear the hammering of the nails and the scraping and clunk of the cross as it is hauled up into position. You hear all the taunts and they pierce you too. How can people be so cruel? And yet when you do risk a glance, Jesus now looks so pathetic. And then it goes dark. You cling to the people you are with, for fear of losing contact in the crowd.

> **[45]** Now from the sixth hour there was darkness over all the land until the ninth hour. **[46]** About the ninth hour Jesus cried with a loud voice, saying, "Eli, Eli, lima sabachthani?" That is, "My God, my God, why have you forsaken me?" Psalm 22:1
>
> **[47]** Some of them who stood there, when they heard it, said, "This man is calling Elijah."
>
> **[48]** Immediately one of them ran and took a sponge, filled it with vinegar, put it on a reed, and gave him a drink. **[49]** The rest said, "Let him be. Let's see whether Elijah comes to save him."
>
> **[50]** Jesus cried again with a loud voice, and yielded up his spirit.
>
> **[51]** Behold, the veil of the temple was torn in two from the top to the bottom. The earth quaked and the rocks were split. **[52]** The tombs were opened, and many bodies of the saints who had fallen asleep

were raised; ⁵³ and coming out of the tombs after his resurrection, they entered into the holy city and appeared to many.

⁵⁴ Now the centurion and those who were with him watching Jesus, when they saw the earthquake and the things that were done, were terrified, saying, "Truly this was the Son of God!"

⁵⁵ Many women were there watching from afar, who had followed Jesus from Galilee, serving him. ⁵⁶ Among them were Mary Magdalene, Mary the mother of James and Joses, and the mother of the sons of Zebedee.

OBSERVATIONS

The grief of watching Jesus die was hard to bear. So was the confusion and doubt that His death engendered. It was ironic that the one person who made a declaration of faith in who He was, immediately on witnessing His death, was a Roman soldier, a Gentile, not one of God's chosen people. Hearing his statement helped to instil a vestige of hope that belief in Jesus as the long-awaited Messiah was somehow not misplaced after all. How tragic that the religious leaders loved God no more than the centurion did and yet were prepared to judge the centurion an outsider and an infidel. Their framework was restricted to a religious institution, plus a desire for a national, independent political identity, when it should have extended to include the whole of creation and life on the earth.

PART 2

JESUS AND HIS FAMILY

7

JESUS' PARENTS WHEN HE WAS TWELVE YEARS OLD

CONTEXT

Jesus grew up in Nazareth, a small village in rural Lower Galilee, about sixteen miles from the Sea of Galilee.[1] He would have lived in a house built of rocks and stones, mortared with mud and coated with clay and having a stone floor. The roof would have been a lattice work of wooden beams, interwoven with branches and palm fronds and covered with hardened mud.[2] His family probably owned about four acres of land on which they would have grown their own food, as this was the usual size of the plots of land belonging to peasants at the time. It was considered that six acres were needed to feed a family, so they would have been poor and very likely struggling to survive.³ This is reflected in the fact that when Jesus was circumcised, Mary and Joseph offered "A pair of turtledoves, or two young pigeons" (Luke 2:24b), as prescribed in the law for those who could not afford a lamb (Leviticus 12:8).

Each morning as He grew up, Jesus would have been used to seeing His mother getting up before dawn to go to the well with the other women to draw water. Once back home, the women would sit down in the communal courtyard to make their daily bread, each pouring a measure of grain from a jar into a grain mill to make flour and then adding to the flour salt, olive oil, water and yeast and kneading it to make dough. This they would roll out into thin, round cakes to be baked in a clay oven and eaten fresh as soon as they were ready. Jesus would reflect this ritual in His prayer "Give us this day our daily bread."⁴

It is tempting to imagine that Jesus' experience of family life would have been fairly benign. However, His relatives were human like us and it might well not have been that simple. The fact that He appears to have lost his earthly father at a young age and the way that His brothers treated Him would tend to support that conjecture.

In the next six sessions we will consider some of the moments in Jesus' life when His family or neighbours approached Him. We do not have any record of Jesus' family instigating conversation with Him when He was a child. However, we do have a record of His parents' reaction to losing Him the moment that He came of age at twelve years old, so that is the subject of this session.

LUKE 2:41-52

QUESTIONS FOR THOUGHT OR DISCUSSION

At whose instigation did Jesus stay behind in Jerusalem?

JESUS' PARENTS WHEN HE WAS TWELVE YEARS OLD

Why do you think that Jesus omitted to tell His parents that He intended to remain in Jerusalem?

What do you think that Jesus hoped to gain from His extended stay in Jerusalem?

How long did Jesus' stay in Jerusalem last?

How did Jesus spend His time on His own in Jerusalem?

What impact did Jesus have on those around Him in the Temple?

What do you notice about Mary's exclamation when she and Joseph found Jesus in the Temple?

What do you notice about Jesus' reply to Mary?

Do you think that Jesus owed His parents an apology?

What did it cost Jesus to return home with His parents?

Who was Jesus showing solidarity with in becoming subject to His parents and going home with them at their bidding?

What does this tell us about Father God?

COMMENTS

Jesus was twelve and had accompanied His parents to the Temple for what, the author imagines, was His Bar Mizpah Ceremony. Afterwards Jesus stayed behind in Jerusalem without telling His parents. It took them a day to realize that He wasn't with other relatives among their extended family and several more days to return to Jerusalem and search for Him. By the time they found Him they were frantic with worry and

Mary landed it on Jesus in no uncertain terms. ""Son!" his mother said to him. "Why have you done this to us? Your father and I have been frantic, searching for you everywhere."" (NLT). She was totally honest, looking to understand, with no condemnation. As far as we know, Jesus did not apologize for causing distress to His parents. If we view Him as mirroring Father God, the logical conclusion is that Father God never promised Mary and Joseph an easy ride. Rather, being willing to suffer for being close to Jesus was part of what He was asking of them. At this point it becomes impossible to look at Jesus only as God. He was at the same time fully human. The author considers that for Jesus to apologize to His parents would have amounted to an expression of dependency and false guilt. Instead, He explained where He was at. Father God was His centre point and at the first opportunity He had, He was seeking to learn all He could from those who knew the Law and the Prophets. We read that the teachers of the Law were amazed at His questions and answers. He must have paid attention to the home schooling He had received and to the teachers in His local synagogue and it would appear that He had the ability to become a high-flying scholar and wanted to learn, if only He could go to school. But His parents could not afford to send Him to school in Jerusalem, He was destined to go into the family business and become a hands-on carpenter. At this point we see Jesus as a human being subjecting Himself to His parents' will and going home with them. He knew what it felt like not to be educated or to fulfil His potential in worldly terms and in that He was identifying Himself with so many others who have suffered the same experience; women in the Muslim world, children in Africa who have to work on the land to survive and whose parents cannot afford the luxury of sending them to school, maybe some of us who missed opportunities when we were younger for whatever reasons. Father God watched it happening to His Son, He knows. Have you ever felt comforted on hearing the words "And me"? The author has! Here we have "And Me" from God, when He could so easily have avoided this level of identification with us. A lack of education did not stop Jesus from fulfilling God's purpose for

His life and very likely spared him from even greater personal pain in His conflict with the Pharisees. This can be a comfort too for anyone who feels as though they have missed opportunities in the past.

MEDITATION

You have just had an unusual week, celebrating the Passover. It has meant the long walk from Nazareth to Jerusalem and possibly camping on the Mount of Olives; an annual pilgrimage that provides a break from the daily routines of rural life. Then remembering the amazing story of Yahweh rescuing your ancestors from Egypt, with signs and wonders and the saving of their eldest sons through the sprinkling of the blood of a lamb on the doorposts of their dwellings. It has been different, stimulating, uplifting, interesting. The Temple has been crowded, as have the narrow streets in Jerusalem. The city is so different from the countryside. And the presence of Yahweh in the Temple compelling and special.

[41] His parents went every year to Jerusalem at the feast of the Passover.

[42] When he was twelve years old, they went up to Jerusalem according to the custom of the feast, [43] and when they had fulfilled the days, as they were returning, the boy Jesus stayed behind in Jerusalem. Joseph and his mother didn't know it, [44] but supposing him to be in the company, they went a day's journey, and they looked for him among their relatives and acquaintances. [45] When they didn't find him, they returned to Jerusalem, looking for him. [46] After three days they found him in the temple, sitting in the middle of the teachers, both listening to them, and asking them questions. [47] All who heard him were amazed at his understanding and his answers. [48] When they saw him, they were astonished, and his mother said to him, "Son, why have you treated us this way? Behold, your father and I were anxiously looking for you."

⁴⁹ He said to them, "Why were you looking for me? Didn't you know that I must be in my Father's house?" ⁵⁰ They didn't understand the saying which he spoke to them. ⁵¹ And he went down with them, and came to Nazareth. He was subject to them, and his mother kept all these sayings in her heart. ⁵² And Jesus increased in wisdom and stature, and in favor with God and men.

OBSERVATIONS

We are told that Jesus amazed the teachers of religious law with His questions and answers. We do not know at what point in His development He became aware of His identity as Messiah, but if as a child, He might well have been desperate to take the first opportunity to explore what that might mean for Him personally. His questions were no academic exercise, they were about His own future.

When Jesus told His parents that He must be about His Father's business, meaning that He needed to understand what the Father had in mind for Him as Messiah, His parents did not understand what He was talking about. How could they? Jesus must have been acutely aware of that and it must have been a lonely place.

For all those who have also felt misunderstood by parents whom they knew did not 'get' who they were, this is another "Me too" identification on Jesus' part.

The dynamic of prayer between Mary and Jesus was along the lines of "God why are you allowing this to happen to me? I can't bear it and I am frantic for it to end." Answer "Don't you know who I am?" This reminds me of what God said to Job, when He refused to explain or defend Himself, although Mary's suffering at this point hardly compares with Job's.

8

JESUS' SECOND COUSIN, JOHN THE BAPTIST

CONTEXT

John the Baptist was born six months before Jesus, to Mary's cousin Elizabeth, so he and Jesus were second cousins. Immediately after John's birth, his father Zechariah prophesied over him:

> [76] "And you, child, will be called a prophet of the Most High;
> for you will go before the face of the Lord to prepare his ways,
>
> [77] to give knowledge of salvation to his people by the remission of their sins,

> ^{78} because of the tender mercy of our God,
>   by which the dawn from on high will visit us,
>
> ^{79} to shine on those who sit in darkness and the shadow of death;
>   to guide our feet into the way of peace."
>
> LUKE 1:76-79

John must have grown up knowing that he had a special ministry to fulfil. He certainly had a clear focus on God's coming action in sending the Messiah, coupled with a passion for declaring God's righteousness and the need for people to turn away from their sins and back to God in readiness. He was outspoken in the way that he did this and showed no fear or respect for persons or their status. After Herod married his half-brother's ex-wife and divorced his first wife, which was against the law in Deuteronomy, John did not hold back in denouncing him. Whether for this reason or because he was afraid of the crowds going out to John and the possibility of an uprising on their part, Herod arrested John and put him in prison. Josephus tells us that John was imprisoned in the citadel of Machaerus, a fortress on the eastern banks of the Dead Sea, not far from where John had been baptizing.[5]

MATTHEW 11:2-15

QUESTIONS FOR THOUGHT OR DISCUSSION

What was prophesied over John when he was a baby?

How and where did John fulfil his calling? (Matthew 3:1-6)

How did people respond to John? (Matthew 3:7-10)

Why was John in prison? (Matthew 14:3-4)

What was John facing in prison? (Matthew 14:5)

How did John respond to the situation?

What would Jesus' reply have meant to John? (Isaiah 35:3-6 and Matthew 11:4-6)

What was the Father asking of John?

What did Jesus say about John? Look up Malachi 3:1.

What does this tell us about the Father's heart for John?

COMMENTS

As with Mary, Father God did not protect John from suffering the consequences of his obedience. Which of us would not be tempted to doubt God and ourselves, faced with solitary confinement and threat of death and the feeling of having been abandoned by God?

John expressed his doubts straight to Jesus and Jesus sent him a reply designed both to comfort and to challenge, roughly quoted from Isaiah 35:5-6 (which was preceded by the encouragement of verses 3-4). John would have recognized the prophecy from Isaiah that Jesus quoted in His reply to him and would have known that it referred to God's coming amongst them. This was a Messianic claim on the part of Jesus, expressed in a way designed not to attract Herod's attention to the fact that Jesus was claiming to be king, given that the messengers were returning to Herod's fortress. The passage was closely linked to Isaiah 50:4-10, where we find another message about opened, listening ears.

The challenge was that John needed to accept the suffering that comes with being loyal to God and to stay loyal.

MEDITATION

Jesus has healed a man with leprosy, a centurion's servant, two demon possessed men, a paralytic, a dead girl, a woman with a haemorrhage, two blind and mute people and many others. He has also calmed a storm on the Sea of Galilee. You are hearing and seeing impossible things, or maybe not. Not much news reaches anyone in prison. John is very likely shackled in a dungeon, with minimal food and water and not much room to move around. He is allowed visitors, however and he sends a delegation to Jesus expressing where he's at.

> [2] Now when John heard in the prison the works of Christ, he sent two of his disciples [3] and said to him, "Are you he who comes, or should we look for another?"
>
> [4] Jesus answered them, "Go and tell John the things which you hear and see: [5] the blind receive their sight, the lame walk, the lepers are cleansed, the deaf hear, Isaiah 35:5 the dead are raised up, and the poor have good news preached to them. Isaiah 61:1-4 [6] Blessed is he who finds no occasion for stumbling in me."
>
> [7] As these went their way, Jesus began to say to the multitudes concerning John, "What did you go out into the wilderness to see? A reed shaken by the wind? [8] But what did you go out to see? A man in soft clothing? Behold, those who wear soft clothing are in kings' houses. [9] But why did you go out? To see a prophet? Yes, I tell you, and much more than a prophet. [10] For this is he, of whom it is written, 'Behold, I send my messenger before your face, who will prepare your way before you.' Malachi 3:1 [11] Most certainly I tell you, among those who are born of women there has not arisen anyone greater than John the Baptizer; yet he who is least in the Kingdom of Heaven is greater than he. [12] From the days of John the Baptizer until now, the Kingdom of Heaven suffers violence, and the violent take it by force. [13] For all the prophets and the law prophesied until John. [14] If you are willing to receive it, this is Elijah, who is to come. [15] He who has ears to hear, let him hear.

OBSERVATIONS

When Jesus asked the people whom they had gone into the wilderness to see, His reference to a weak reed might well have been an allusion to Herod's coinage, which featured a reed as an emblem. If so, Jesus is making the point that from His perspective as God, Herod's power was not that great.

Even so, John the Baptist paid for his outspokenness with his life and without even a trial. It is as though Jesus' message back to John was implying that death was less of an issue than disobedience or disbelief.

9

JESUS' MOTHER AND BROTHERS

CONTEXT

Jesus travelled around the hills and villages of Galilee, teaching in the synagogues, on the hills and from boats on the Sea of Galilee that the Kingdom of God had come near. He healed a great many people and word had spread. Nearly everywhere He went a large crowd followed Him. Both when His disciples plucked ears of corn while walking through a field on the Sabbath and when Jesus healed a man with a shrivelled hand in the synagogue on the Sabbath, the Pharisees contested Him for breaking the law and for allowing His disciples to do the same. Jesus defended both Himself and His disciples by indicating that He was Lord of the Sabbath and in so doing implied that He was the Messiah. This offended the Pharisees and they started plotting to kill Jesus. Jesus was aware of this and withdrew, but the crowds and the Pharisees followed Him.

The description that we have of Jesus' mother and brothers arriving at the edge of the crowd wanting to speak to Him is included by both Mark (Mark 3:31-35) and Luke (Luke 8:19-21). Mark previously included a comment that Jesus' family already considered Him to be "out of his mind," (Mark 3:21 NLT) and had tried to take charge of Him. Matthew says nothing of that, but it would seem fair to conclude from Jesus' response to His family's presence that they still considered Him out of His mind and wanted to take charge of Him.

MATTHEW 12:46-50

QUESTIONS FOR THOUGHT OR DISCUSSION

How important were family ties in Jesus' day?

What has Jesus already done to risk His place in His family dynamic?

What implications, if any, might Jesus' choices have had for His family?

Why were Jesus' family asking to speak with Him?

What was Jesus' response regarding His family?

What does Jesus' response regarding His family tell us about His priorities?

What does verse 50 tell us about how Jesus viewed His followers?

What does verse 50 mean for Jesus' followers today?

What does Jesus' response tell us about how Father God saw the situation?

What does Jesus' response imply about how Father God sees Jesus' followers today?

COMMENTS

We do not know what Jesus' mother and brothers would have said to Him had they been able to get near enough to interact with Him. Maybe they had heard that the Pharisees were plotting to kill Jesus and were concerned that He might not know, so they had come to warn Him. Maybe they were afraid that if Jesus' life was in danger, so were theirs, so they wanted to take Him home and persuade Him to give up teaching. Maybe they were missing His input on their land and in the workshop. He had certainly broken with family tradition and cultural norms leaving home like He had. Maybe they just could not compute that someone as close to them as He was could really be the Messiah and that therefore He must be a megalomaniac to think that of Himself, as He clearly did. Either way it would appear that they had every intention of controlling Him into silence.

We can only infer, from Jesus' response to being told that His family had come, that He knew why they had come and that whatever they wanted to say would not have been affirmative of either Him or His ministry. At first sight Jesus' response to their coming might appear rather dismissive and disrespectful, especially towards His mother. However, we have already seen, when Jesus was only twelve, that His primary focus was on doing His heavenly Father's will. The fact that His family wanted to close down His ministry showed little or no respect for who He really was and they reaped accordingly, although He did not repudiate them for it.

In declining to be silenced, even by His immediate family, Jesus made what must have seemed an astonishing claim, declaring His disciples to be His mother and His brothers, those doing the will of His Father in heaven. In so doing He severed Himself from His family and placed His primary loyalty with Father God. For anyone whose family disowns them for being a follower of Jesus, this amounts to another "Me too" moment on Jesus' part. Then He invited anyone who was willing to do what His Father wants to become His brother and sister and mother, or in other words, everything to Him. His invitation potentially included even the Pharisees and actually specified women, which was utterly counter cultural.

This passage implies a couple of challenging questions. Are we willing to follow Jesus and not to cave in, faced with opposition? If that is the case, Jesus owns us as His family. As such, do we see ourselves as more closely related to Jesus and to fellow followers of Jesus than to our blood family, whether or not faced with a conflict of loyalty?

MEDITATION

Jesus has withdrawn from the place where He had healed a man with a withered hand in the synagogue on the Sabbath. He is walking through the countryside and enters a friend's house, where there is a courtyard with room for a large crowd of people to follow Him inside. Many are doing so, crowding into the restricted space to make room for as many people as possible. Among the people there are His close friends and those supporting Him, peasants from the local area wanting to understand what is going on, sick people hoping to be healed and some Pharisees, from whom Jesus had been hoping to escape. He is continuing to teach, there is so much that He wants the people to know.

> [46] While he was yet speaking to the multitudes, behold, his mother and his brothers stood outside, seeking to speak to him. [47] One said to him, "Behold, your mother and your brothers stand outside, seeking to speak to you."

> [48] But he answered him who spoke to him, "Who is my mother? Who are my brothers?" [49] He stretched out his hand toward his disciples, and said, "Behold, my mother and my brothers! [50] For whoever does the will of my Father who is in heaven, he is my brother, and sister, and mother."

OBSERVATIONS

Jesus was not for being manipulated or controlled. His loyalty was first and foremost to Father God and only secondarily to His earthly family. He knew the cost and earned the right to say to His followers that they needed to be prepared to put God above earthly ties if they wanted to follow Him.

His mother and brothers met with a blank wall when they tried to close Jesus down. If our prayers feel like they are hitting the ceiling and bouncing off, maybe we need to ask ourselves whether we are trying to manipulate God. We can be sure that it won't work; He is bound to be true to Himself.

It must grieve the Father's heart to watch the church proclaiming herself to be family, but too often not delivering on what that really means in practice.

10

JESUS' NEIGHBOURS IN NAZARETH

CONTEXT
Jesus was moving around Galilee, teaching about the Kingdom. He was repeatedly put under pressure by the Pharisees and He repeatedly moved on to evade them. In one place they accused Jesus of casting out demons by the prince of demons and in another they asked to see a miraculous sign. Jesus gave quite stringent responses on both occasions, making no bones about the fact that they belonged to a wicked generation, who would be condemned by their own words. He refused to be silenced by His family, instead proceeding to teach about the Kingdom in terms of parables about weeds and pearls. Yet again He moved on and came

to Nazareth, where He grew up. It was a small and unremarkable village, about sixteen miles from the Sea of Galilee. He had lived there for many years, so would have known everyone there quite well, and been known well by them in return. A happy and joyful reunion one might imagine, but for the fact that Luke records Jesus returning there straight after His baptism by John and the people of Nazareth attempting to throw Him off a cliff. That might explain why Jesus and His mother and brothers no longer lived there. His sisters would have been married by then, with no choice but to stay and we can imagine were therefore present in the synagogue.

MATTHEW 13:53-58

QUESTIONS FOR THOUGHT OR DISCUSSION

What did the people of Nazareth know about Jesus?

Why might the people of Nazareth have wanted to throw Jesus off a cliff immediately on His return from being baptized? (Luke 4:14-30)

Why would Jesus want to return to Nazareth?

What do you think Jesus might have said when He was teaching in the synagogue?

Why were the people of Nazareth offended by Jesus?

Why was it so difficult for the people of Nazareth to believe that Jesus was who He said He was, ie the Messiah?

What impact would the people of Nazareth's attitude to Jesus have had on Jesus' family?

How did Jesus respond to the people of Nazareth?

What does this tell us about Father God's heart for the people of Nazareth?

COMMENTS

The villagers in Nazareth had watched Jesus growing up and thought they knew who He was. They were over familiar and threatened by His superior knowledge of God and ability to perform miracles. After all, if Him then why not them? That would have been an uncomfortable comparison. Too uncomfortable, for we read that they refused to believe who He really was. How did He respond? With restraint and none of the powerful works that He must have been longing to do for those who needed them.

The author would like to think that she might have more in common with Jesus' disciples than with some of the other groups of people who approached Him. However, when it comes to the failure of Jesus' fellow villagers to believe in His power, I have to confess a level of identification. You may have seen some of the long Covid-19 sufferers on the news, the ones who have not recovered after months of illness. One woman in particular said that she was spending all her time out of work recovering from having been at work and had no other life and no clue about how long it would be for, as there is no cure. She reminded me of when I had Glandular Fever for nearly nine years, as my experience for much of that time was similar to hers. By the end of that time, I had forgotten what it was like to be well and could not even imagine it. I had no faith in Jesus' power to heal me, in spite of the fact that He had twice given me a promise from Isaiah 40:31:

> "…but those who wait for Yahweh will renew their strength.
> They will mount up with wings like eagles.
> They will run, and not be weary.
> They will walk, and not faint."

I had so little belief that the first time I was given that promise I forgot about it altogether. Jesus in His mercy did heal me, but it was largely in response to the faith of others, not my own faith. A friend took me to a healing conference and one of the team looked me straight in the eye at the beginning of the week and said: "Jesus is going to heal you this week." I looked straight back at her and said nothing. I was thinking, "I cannot say yes, because I don't believe it, so I'd be lying. But I refuse to say no, so I can't say anything." There followed lots of challenges requiring me to repent and renounce ungodly attitudes and actions in order to clear the ground and it was only when the leader of the ministry stood up to preach later in the week and announced that the text for her talk that evening was from Isaiah 40: "Those who wait for Yahweh will renew their strength. They will mount up with wings like eagles. They will run and not be weary. They will walk and not faint" that I was suddenly able to believe that the time for me to be healed had come. It was a case of faith comes by hearing and hearing by the word of God. It was pure gift. If God or His power seem distant, we may need to consider our attitude towards Him as a possible reason.

MEDITATION

You are living in Galilee, a rural area, mostly cultivated by subsistence farmers growing their own food, as do you. The terrain is gently undulating, there are few roads and most people travel on foot. In summer the ground is dusty and what grass remains is yellow from the effect of the sun. In spring the grass is green and there are wild flowers everywhere, giving a brief blaze of colour. You have grown up with Jesus and His brothers and sisters, in a small and not very well-known village. His sisters are all married and living locally still. Jesus and His mother and brothers have moved away, but you keep hearing reports that Jesus has been travelling around Galilee healing people and drawing crowds. It all sounds a bit unlikely. He was such an ordinary guy, or so you thought. Yes, you held him in favour, He was an exemplary Jew, but He was also a peasant like you. Now at last He is staying in the village and it is very likely that He will be teaching in the synagogue. This is a good chance to see what all the fuss is about, an opportunity not to be missed.

> [53] When Jesus had finished these parables, he departed from there. [54] Coming into his own country, he taught them in their synagogue, so that they were astonished and said, "Where did this man get this wisdom and these mighty works? [55] Isn't this the carpenter's son? Isn't his mother called Mary, and his brothers James, Joses, Simon and Judas? [56] Aren't all of his sisters with us? Where then did this man get all of these things?" [57] They were offended by him.
>
> But Jesus said to them, "A prophet is not without honor, except in his own country and in his own house." [58] He didn't do many mighty works there because of their unbelief.

OBSERVATIONS

It was hard for the people of Nazareth, who thought they knew who Jesus was, to compute the difference between how they saw Him and how He clearly saw Himself. How could He possibly be the long-awaited Messiah? It was too huge to take in. And where had He learned so many things so far beyond their normal horizon? It was too much of a challenge to face.

Jesus showed enormous restraint and respect even, in withdrawing and not foisting His power to work miracles onto them. He also demonstrated courage in remaining true to Himself, declaring Himself to be a prophet despite His neighbours' resistance to the idea. He never shirked in giving feedback about what He saw in people; in this case the refusal of His family and those in His hometown to honour Him as a prophet being in stark contrast to the honour that He was receiving in other places.

11

JESUS' BROTHERS

CONTEXT

John's Gospel has a rather different timeline from Matthew's, as it is organized around the Jewish festivals to highlight theological truths, rather than around events in their historical order.

John describes Jesus travelling to Judea and being baptized, then back to Galilee where He turned water into wine at a wedding in Cana. Then back to Jerusalem for the Passover and a subsequent stay in Judea, where Jesus' disciples were baptizing people. When Jesus heard that the Pharisees had become aware that His disciples were baptizing more people than John the Baptist was, He returned to Galilee via

JESUS' BROTHERS

Samaria. There followed another miracle in Cana and another trip to Jerusalem for a one-day festival, during which Jesus healed someone on the Sabbath. This led to objections from the Pharisees, which were intensified when Jesus defended Himself by claiming to be one with the Father. The Pharisees recognized this as a claim to be equal with God and started plotting to kill Jesus. Jesus therefore withdrew to Galilee and taught in the villages there, until it was time for the Festival of Shelters, or Tabernacles.

JOHN 7:1-10

QUESTIONS FOR THOUGHT OR DISCUSSION

How many brothers did Jesus have? (Matthew 13:55)

How much time would Jesus and His brothers have spent together as children?

What do you think might have contributed to distance between Jesus and His brothers as they have grown older? (Luke 4:14-16 & 28-30)

What feelings do you think Jesus' brothers might have had towards Him?

Where were Jesus' brothers coming from in verses 3-4?

What must family life have felt like for Jesus?

How did Jesus handle the difficulties in His family relationships?

Where was Jesus coming from in His reply to His brothers in verses 6-8?

What might Jesus' motives have been for going to the festival separately from His bothers?

What does Jesus' directness with His brothers about the difference between Himself and the world (including them) tell us about the Father's heart towards Jesus' brothers?

COMMENTS

Jesus' brothers taunted Him that He should go up to Jerusalem for the Festival of Tabernacles publicly, despite the opposition they all knew He would face. Jesus knew their hearts and their refusal to recognize who He was and declined to go with them. He told His brothers that the world had no reason to hate them, but that it hated Him because He testified of it that its works were evil. Then He withdrew from them. Was that for His safety from the authorities? Or for His brothers' safety, that they not be seen associated with Him? Or to save Himself from their ridicule? It must have hurt. But Jesus' reply to them was not designed to protect Himself, it was quite blunt and offensive. "The world can't hate you but it does hate me because I accuse it of sin and evil." It is likely that Jesus wanted to get His brothers to realize that they needed to change their approach if they were to experience the fellowship with Father God that He so enjoyed and longed for them to enter. Letting them go without Him must have been gutting. Then Jesus went up to the festival in secret and apart from His family. This mirrored the fact that Father God never pushes Himself in where He is not wanted. Jesus' appearance in public part-way through the festival was not designed to protect Himself either, although the short notice would have reduced the chance that it gave the Jewish leaders to organize His death.

MEDITATION

Jesus and His brothers grew up together. There were five of them and most, if not all, of the younger ones were probably born in Nazareth. They would have slept, together with their parents, in a simple, stone flagged dwelling, very likely arranged around a courtyard surrounded by other dwellings where their relatives lived. They would have worked in the fields together, along with their cousins and played together once the work was done.

Childhood is now long gone. Jesus' claims to be the Messiah have resulted in all the brothers needing to leave Nazareth, along with their mother. It is likely that they have settled in Capernaum, on the shore of the Sea of Galilee, but the dislocation has been costly. As good Jews, Jesus' brothers travel to Jerusalem regularly to attend the festivals. They are busy getting ready for another trip to Jerusalem. Are their sandals in good repair? They have a long walk ahead of them. Bag with sleeping mat in case they have to camp, flint with which to light fires to keep themselves safe overnight, bag of silver coins with which to buy food on the journey. Jesus does not appear to be getting ready to travel and His brothers cannot resist having a go at Him before they set out. It's not their fault that Jesus has been crazy enough to upset the Pharisees so much.

> 7 After these things, Jesus was walking in Galilee, for he wouldn't walk in Judea, because the Jews sought to kill him. ² Now the feast of the Jews, the Feast of Booths, was at hand. ³ His brothers therefore said to him, "Depart from here and go into Judea, that your disciples also may see your works which you do. ⁴ For no one does anything in secret while he seeks to be known openly. If you do these things, reveal yourself to the world." ⁵ For even his brothers didn't believe in him.
>
> ⁶ Jesus therefore said to them, "My time has not yet come, but your time is always ready. ⁷ The world can't hate you, but it hates me, because I testify about it, that its works are evil. ⁸ You go up to the feast. I am not yet going up to this feast, because my time is not yet fulfilled."
>
> ⁹ Having said these things to them, he stayed in Galilee. ¹⁰ But when his brothers had gone up to the feast, then he also went up, not publicly, but as it were in secret.

OBSERVATIONS

Thinking about the dynamic between Jesus and His brothers from the perspective of a brother, it was actually quite annoying to be told that I was evil and Jesus wasn't, I felt angry. I am always in the wrong and God is always in the right!

Then it occurred to me that Jesus' brothers were accusing Jesus of wanting the limelight, which wasn't true. Jesus wanted to show the Father to people and for His brothers, along with everyone else, to be reconciled with the Father. Jesus' brothers were very likely afraid of the authorities and were maligning Jesus to justify themselves and that was upsetting. In leaving His brothers to go to the festival without Him, Jesus was shielding them from danger through association with Himself and responding to the fear that He knew was behind their ridicule. Even when hurt by them, He was thinking of their welfare above His own.

12

MARY, THE MOTHER OF JESUS, AT THE CROSS

CONTEXT

Jesus and His disciples were in Jerusalem for the Passover. We know that His mother was there and it is likely that His brothers were there too. John was known to the staff at the house of Caiaphas, the high priest, which could have been due to the fact that he regularly delivered fish there and/or that he was of priestly descent and sometimes officiated in the Temple. In the light of that it would not have been surprising if John's parents Zebedee and Salome, (who some think was Mary's sister) had a house in Jerusalem. If so, it would have been quite natural for Mary to be staying with her sister Salome, along with Joseph's brother

Cleopas and his wife "the other Mary."[6]

We do not know where nine of the disciples went from the Garden of Gethsemane after Jesus' arrest. The natural line of retreat away from danger would have been towards Bethany, to tell Mary and Martha. We do know that John and Peter did not take that route, as they were together in the courtyard of Caiaphas, where they were able to witness part of Jesus' trial. From there they, or at least John, would have been able to return to John's home in Jerusalem to tell his parents and Jesus' mother what had happened.

The next day Mary was at the foot of the cross, where she must have been allowed close access by the centurion shortly after Jesus was crucified. With her were her sister Salome, sister-in-law Mary, Mary Magdalene (who may have been Martha's sister, now living locally in Bethany)[7] and nephew John.

JOHN 19:25-27

QUESTIONS FOR THOUGHT OR DISCUSSION

In what ways had God prepared Mary for what happened to Jesus? (Luke 2:33-35, Matthew 2:9-11)

Do you think that having heard Simeon and met the Magi, Mary would have expected Jesus to die in the way that He did?

What was the significance of being hung on a tree in the minds of first century Jews? (Galatians 3:13)

What do you imagine Mary was going through, seeing Jesus dying on a cross?

What were the potential implications for her personally?

MARY, THE MOTHER OF JESUS, AT THE CROSS

What did Mary's presence at the cross communicate to Jesus?

What resulted for Mary from her being so close to the foot of the cross?

What does this tell us about Father God's heart for her?

What does it tell us about what to expect as disciples of Jesus?

COMMENTS

We do not have any words from Mary recorded at the scene of Jesus' crucifixion. Mary's very presence there was a silent prayer that spoke volumes, even while she was quite likely completely beyond words. Jesus' death this way was not supposed to happen. She must have been dying inside herself, watching her first-born son die the agonizing and slow death of a convicted criminal, on public display for all to see. However, she did not allow the ignominy of the situation to keep her away. She was there to support Jesus to the end and to know what happened to Him. And her presence in His presence did not escape His notice. It must have been a big comfort to Him that she was there, as well as hard to watch her suffering on His account. Despite His own unimaginable suffering, Jesus responded to Mary's need in love and gave her John as her new son, to support her from then on. One must wonder where His brothers were at that point, but John was there, alone among the disciples. If it is true that John was Jesus' cousin, then Mary would have been his aunt and he was there supporting her. Jesus wanted to be sure that His mother would be provided for and knew that John loved Him enough not to let Him or her down. John was within earshot and listening for anything Jesus had to say, His precious last words, not to be missed. Maybe he was asking himself what he could do to help. Jesus did not need him to say anything, He knew, as did Father God and He responded with His request for help for His mother. He might have involved Mary in unimaginable suffering, but He loved her completely.

It is quite possible that John took Mary home at that point, early on before the darkness fell and then spent some considerable time with her at his home, before he returned himself to the scene of the crucifixion, where he heard and remembered some of the later words of Jesus from the cross.[8]

MEDITATION

There is tension in the air. You have not felt this level of foreboding before. Jerusalem is packed with people, but that is nothing new. You have seen it all before at previous festivals. Accommodation in short supply. Food overpriced. The Temple overcrowded. Pilate fearing a riot. If Caesar hears of it, as he surely would, it would be banishment for Pilate and the garrison. The Roman soldiers fear it too. The Jewish leaders fear the Romans razing the Temple to the ground. The Jewish people fear Yahweh's displeasure. Jesus' family fear for His future and for their own. Their fears are the first to be realized. Can this really be Jesus emerging from the Antonia Fortress, dragging a cross on his bloodied back? That can only mean one thing. He is barely recognizable. You cannot take your eyes off Him, although you can barely bear to look, as you jostle with the crowd to keep up with where He's being taken. You do not want to lose Him. Along the narrow streets you know so well, through the gate in the city wall, out onto a mound near the road from Jericho to the coast. Well placed for passers-by to see what's happened. The soldiers stop and strip Jesus. Every blow of their mallet goes right through you. You cannot look. Then a loud clunk. This cannot be real. All hope now gone. You go numb.

> [25] But standing by Jesus' cross were his mother, his mother's sister, Mary the wife of Clopas, and Mary Magdalene. [26] Therefore when Jesus saw his mother, and the disciple whom he loved standing there, he said to his mother, "Woman, behold, your son!" [27] Then he said to the disciple, "Behold, your mother!" From that hour, the disciple took her to his own home.

OBSERVATIONS

Mary would have been destitute without the support of a male relative. At the cross she was in need of emotional support, as well as a source of provision for the future. Mary almost certainly did not have a base in Jerusalem, but being adopted into John's family would have meant that she acquired one, without having needed to ask for it. The fact that Jesus instigated her adoption meant that she did not have to feel guilty about being a burden. If John was accepting her into his family for Jesus, then she was free to receive the provision as from Him.

Being loved by God does not guarantee that we are protected from suffering at the hands of other people. However, we can be sure that God is aware of our suffering and is keen to provide for us. Mary staying close to Jesus, even when He was being crucified, meant that she was within earshot of God's provision for her and John being there meant that he was within earshot of Jesus' request for his help. She was losing a son and Jesus provided her with an adoptive son, a family to belong to and the provision of food and a home for the future. Her sons did not have the love for Jesus at this point that she and John had and it is probable that they did not have a base in Jerusalem. They were no-where to be seen, just when Mary needed them most.

PART 3

JESUS AND HIS DISCIPLES

13

"SAVE US, LORD! WE ARE DYING!"

CONTEXT

We do not know whether the disciples who had been fishermen got into the boat with Jesus, but it is very likely that they did. Nor do we know whether they were able to predict the freak and dangerous storms for which the Sea of Galilee is famous. Probably not. Either way, Jesus got into a boat and some or all of the disciples followed Him. Jesus must have been exhausted. Prior to crossing the lake He had taught a large crowd of people the Sermon on the Mount, descended the mountain, healed a leper, walked to Capernaum, healed a centurion's servant, healed Peter's mother-in-law, healed numerous people from Capernaum who appeared outside the house on hearing the news of Peter's mother-in-law and then found Himself surrounded by yet more crowds. He needed to get away from the crowds and their demands and decided to escape across the lake. On the way to the boat, He responded to two more people who managed to get to the front of the crowds and ask Him questions. Then He embarked and fell fast asleep in the stern of the boat.

MATTHEW 8:23-27

QUESTIONS FOR THOUGHT OR DISCUSSION

Who could the disciples have appealed to for help when the storm arose?

Why did the disciples wake Jesus up?

Why did the disciples, several of whom were experienced fishermen, appeal to Jesus to save them?

What do you think the disciples expected Jesus to be able to do?

How would you have reacted if asked to save the disciples in such a storm?

How did Jesus react?

What does Jesus' response imply about His identity?

Given that the disciples didn't yet realize who Jesus was, why did He call them "O you of little faith"? (Literally "little faiths" in the Greek).

What does this incident tell us about the Father heart of God?

"SAVE US, LORD! WE ARE DYING!"

COMMENTS

Jesus' choice of disciples was interesting. He picked ordinary working men; people who had failed to be picked by other rabbis as likely to benefit from an academic education. Among them was a guy who had sold out to the Roman domination and become a tax collector, at least he could make good money that way. Alongside him was a Zealot, who would gladly have joined any insurrection aimed at overthrowing the Romans and to whom anyone collecting taxes for them would surely have seemed a traitor. Then there were three of Jesus' cousins, James son of Cleopas on His father's side and James and John, sons of Zebedee and Salome on His mother's side.[1] They were close to Him and from His local community and peasant strata of society. Conspicuous by their absence was anyone from the religious hierarchy.

Jesus' disciples would have been used to attending synagogue worship Sabbath by Sabbath. They would have heard the story of their ancestors being rescued from Egypt and exiled to Babylon, along with the messages of the prophets promising a Messiah. They were Jews and therefore believers in Yahweh. However, it becomes apparent on the lake that they were unbelieving believers. None of them appears to have called on Yahweh to save them when it came to needing a miracle on account of the storm. Instead, they were terrified and woke Jesus up, despite not yet believing that He was the Messiah.

It is interesting to speculate on why the disciples woke Jesus. We are given to believe that they had reached the end of their own resources, because they did not only wake Jesus up because they thought He needed to be aware of what was happening, they appealed to Him to save them. Was that because He had got them into this mess? The author finds it intriguing that experienced fishermen were appealing to Jesus for help, when they knew perfectly well that He was not an experienced sailor. Maybe they were just expecting Him to muck in and pull His weight in trying to control the boat. Or maybe having watched Him healing so many people miraculously they were thinking: "If anyone can do anything now, it's got to be Him." It is likely that they all knew of people who had drowned in similar circumstances on the lake and that if the boat went down, they had no chance of survival, as the lake was too big and too rough to swim across and there were no rescue services.

Jesus picked up on the disciples' fear. He asked them: "Why are you fearful?" and called them "little faiths!" Jesus was a local and would have been aware of the happenings on the lake. His question might appear to be directed at the disciples' view of Him. "Why are you afraid given that I am here with you?" On the other hand, He knew that the disciples had not yet recognized who He was. In calling the disciples "little faiths," He was likely referring to their failure to appeal to Yahweh, who after all was the only person who would be able to control a storm. He might as well have said: "What are you asking me for?" But He didn't. He responded to their request to be saved by doing exactly what only Yahweh had the power to do; He arose, rebuked the wind and the sea and there was a great calm. The disciples weren't expecting that! We read that they were amazed and started asking themselves the obvious question: "What kind of man is this, that even the wind and the sea obey him?"

The disciples' expectation of Jesus did not limit His response, He responded because they approached Him for help. Just the fact that they had asked Him to save them was enough for Him to respond with what was needed, way beyond their expectations of what was possible. But not only that, in doing what only God could do, He was demonstrating His true identity to them. That could be why He did not ask the disciples why they were appealing to Him. In fact, they were appealing to the right person after all!

MEDITATION

Life has turned into a roller coaster since you started following Jesus around the place. You never know what is going to happen next and there has been little time to eat or sleep lately. Jesus is exhausted and in need of a rest. However, that is difficult to come by on land, as people keep on seeking Him out. Out on the lake is a much better bet. Or so it seemed. Jesus has embarked across the lake in a local fishing boat, probably belonging to the family of one of the disciples. The fishermen among them are able to take it out; they know exactly what they are doing. To start with all seems well with the weather and Jesus grabs the opportunity for the rest He so badly needs and falls fast asleep in the stern of the boat. You aim for the far shore. And then the calm and pleasant journey turns into a nightmare, as one of the dreaded storms suddenly and unexpectedly blows up from nowhere in a matter of minutes.

> [23] When he got into a boat, his disciples followed him. [24] Behold, a violent storm came up on the sea, so much that the boat was covered with the waves; but he was asleep. [25] The disciples came to him and woke him up, saying, "Save us, Lord! We are dying!"
>
> [26] He said to them, "Why are you fearful, O you of little faith?" Then he got up, rebuked the wind and the sea, and there was a great calm.
>
> [27] The men marveled, saying, "What kind of man is this, that even the wind and the sea obey him?"

OBSERVATIONS

Even after reading the Comments section, I did not think to pray to Yahweh for help when in the boat with Jesus and the others. I was angry that Jesus wasn't doing anything because He was asleep, as well as being frightened and then still frightened when it became calm. That led to a conversation with Jesus about wanting to be able to control Him, in order to feel safe. It amounted to wishing to be God, rather than having to trust Him. Time for growth! Then I realized that my feelings reflected those that I had experienced in a sailing accident that had nearly cost me my life. I was projecting them on to Jesus without being aware of it all these years later. Time for healing of the memory.

14

"WHY DO YOU SPEAK TO THEM IN PARABLES?"

CONTEXT

After Jesus had calmed a storm on the lake, He and the disciples reached the far shore, where Jesus proceeded to heal a couple of demon possessed people. Then Jesus and His disciples returned back across the lake to more familiar surroundings. Jesus healed many sick and demon possessed people, called Matthew to be a disciple, sent the twelve disciples out in pairs to drive out demons and heal the sick themselves and responded to John the Baptist's messengers. Then He upset the Pharisees by doing good on the Sabbath and declined to be silenced by His family, proclaiming those who do the will of His Father in heaven

"WHY DO YOU SPEAK TO THEM IN PARABLES?"

as His true family, pointing to His disciples.

In the disciples we see a group of people who ate, slept, lived and travelled together with Jesus, truly his newly adopted family. They were close enough to Jesus to experience a rather different kind of life from the one they had been used to and to find themselves frequently unable to make Him out. They were also close enough to be able to ask their questions and ask them they did. The answers to the questions they asked were not always comfortable listening, however. Even when they were told how privileged they were compared with others, they still found themselves being challenged. The private conversation between Jesus and the disciples, after Jesus had told the story of the Sower going out to sow, is a case in point.

MATTHEW 13:10-23

QUESTIONS FOR THOUGHT OR DISCUSSION

How do you think the disciples might have felt about being unable to understand the meaning of Jesus' parables?

What do you think the disciples really wanted to know when they asked Jesus why He spoke in parables so often? Was it that or something else?

If something else, why did the disciples ask the question they asked and not the question to which they really wanted to know the answer?

Given the disciples' question was phrased quite negatively, what do you notice about Jesus' response?

What does this tell us about the Father heart of God?

Think of someone you know who doesn't know Jesus.

What modern day story could you use to point them to Jesus?

What spiritual truth does your story convey?

COMMENTS

The disciples could not understand why Jesus was telling parables. The implication is that the disciples thought that Jesus' stories were cryptic and difficult to understand. They were taken from everyday life and would have been familiar scenarios to Jesus' listeners and easy to remember. But the disciples, it seems, suspected that Jesus was getting at something deeper and could not fathom it out. Rather than admitting that and asking what the parable meant, they asked a rather more oblique question about why Jesus was being so cryptic. In other words, how could they be expected to understand?! Maybe they were feeling threatened by their inability to 'get' it on their own. Maybe they felt insecure on account of being at the bottom of the pile academically and knowing it. They would not have wanted to admit their insecurity if they did not feel good about it, so they projected their negativity onto Jesus with a barbed question that amounted to a complaint about His teaching style. This would not have been lost on Jesus, but He responded by answering the question that they actually asked Him. In His answer the author believes that we see the heart of the Father never to pressurise anyone into acknowledging Him. All Jesus' stories were really about spiritual truths for those who would face them, told in such a way as to be memorable but also ignorable.

Having answered the question that the disciples asked, Jesus proceeded to answer the question that He perceived they were really wanting to ask, about what on earth did the parable of the Sower mean. Jesus heard the disciples' diffidence about not being able to work it out for themselves and probably felt their frustration with Him for telling parables all the time. Many people would be tempted to respond to a put down with a defensive put down of their own in return, but not Jesus. He began His answer with an affirmation of the disciples' status in His sight. Not everyone would be getting to hear what it meant, but they would, by virtue of their closeness to Him. How gracious Jesus was! Then He explained the parable in terms of a challenge to act on the word that He was sowing by putting Father God first and foremost in the face of every kind of temptation not to, which He had the right to say as it was how He lived. Think back to when He was twelve years old in the Temple with the religious leaders, seeking to understand the Father's will for his life. Father God so longs to have His rightful place in our hearts so that we can discover what it means to live as we were created to live, in unbroken fellowship with Him. Jesus was modelling that as a human being and also reflecting Father God's heart in the way that He treated the disciples. At the same time, He was challenging the disciples that to be fruitful they would need to hold on to His teaching, keep holding on when the going would get tough and not let anything compete with the Father for first place in the affection of their hearts. The aim being that they would indeed bear much fruit.

The author tried telling stories to her students when she was a lecturer and reference to God or Jesus was not politically correct. I was in a situation in which the students were feeling let down by a changed circumstance that was beyond the control of the lecturing team. I felt that the students were in danger of wasting energy complaining about something that was not rectifiable. I told them a story about treasure in a purse that they had to find buried underneath a boulder and thus challenged them to rise above the current difficulty they were facing and to keep focussed on their studies. They did! But what I found interesting watching their response was that to me the treasure in the purse was Jesus and to the students it was succeeding in getting their degree and Social Work qualification. I had to watch on and stick to story level communication, much as Jesus did with the crowds in His day. I can only hope and pray that if Social Work does not retain its pearl-like status, the students will remember the story and have cause to wonder what else the treasure might represent.

MEDITATION

Earlier today you have heard Jesus telling the crowds that He views His disciples as His real family, along with anyone who does the Father's will. You are stunned, as family ties are sacrosanct in your culture. All in the same day Jesus has got into a boat and told stories to those on the shore, including about a Sower sowing his seed. That is such a familiar scenario. When you haven't been planting your own crops, you have seen others planting theirs. Jesus' description of the wastage rings so true, as does His description of variable yields. But what is He driving at? There must be more to it than meets the eye, or Jesus would not be bothering to tell the story. You still have not 'got' it when all the crowds have gone, so you grab your chance to ask Jesus privately.

> [10] The disciples came, and said to him, "Why do you speak to them in parables?"
>
> [11] He answered them, "To you it is given to know the mysteries of the Kingdom of Heaven, but it is not given to them. [12] For whoever has, to him will be given, and he will have abundance; but whoever doesn't have, from him will be taken away even that which he has. [13] Therefore I speak to them in parables, because seeing they don't see, and hearing, they don't hear, neither do they understand. [14] In them the prophecy of Isaiah is fulfilled, which says,
>
> > 'By hearing you will hear,
> >   and will in no way understand;
> > Seeing you will see,
> >   and will in no way perceive;
> > [15] for this people's heart has grown callous,
> >   their ears are dull of hearing,
> >   and they have closed their eyes;

"WHY DO YOU SPEAK TO THEM IN PARABLES?"

> or else perhaps they might perceive with their eyes,
>> hear with their ears,
>> understand with their heart,
> and would turn again,
>> and I would heal them.' Isaiah 6:9-10

[16] "But blessed are your eyes, for they see; and your ears, for they hear. [17] For most certainly I tell you that many prophets and righteous men desired to see the things which you see, and didn't see them; and to hear the things which you hear, and didn't hear them.

[18] "Hear, then, the parable of the farmer. [19] When anyone hears the word of the Kingdom and doesn't understand it, the evil one comes and snatches away that which has been sown in his heart. This is what was sown by the roadside. [20] What was sown on the rocky places, this is he who hears the word and immediately with joy receives it; [21] yet he has no root in himself, but endures for a while. When oppression or persecution arises because of the word, immediately he stumbles. [22] What was sown among the thorns, this is he who hears the word, but the cares of this age and the deceitfulness of riches choke the word, and he becomes unfruitful. [23] What was sown on the good ground, this is he who hears the word and understands it, who most certainly bears fruit and produces, some one hundred times as much, some sixty, and some thirty."

OBSERVATIONS

This dialogue produced a roller-coaster of emotions. First of all frustration at not being able to understand. Then a feeling of why me, why am I so special? Then grief that so many were missing out. Then anticipation and excitement at being about to hear the truth from Jesus. Then the challenge to put God first.

And then the question: "How would Jesus have framed His stories for a modern world?" It is worth asking Him. When I did so I received the following, which I then realized perfectly fitted a friend's situation.

"A friend was going on a journey. They filled their car up with petrol, piled their luggage into the boot and then set off all in a rush, as they were due to meet with a dignitary and were worried about being late. The result was that they forgot the Sat Nav and didn't have a map with them either. Quite early in the journey they took a wrong turning and ended up completely lost. They passed a few people and stopped to ask the way, but none of them knew the way to where my friend was going. Eventually they saw a hitchhiker, whom they would normally have passed by on principle. However, this hitchhiker was displaying a sign showing my friend's destination, so they stopped and invited the stranger into the car. From that moment on the journey started to feel quite different. The stranger was gracious and polite and knew exactly where they needed to be going. Every time they reached a junction and my friend didn't know which way to turn, the stranger did. They arrived at my friend's destination with minutes to spare before the start of the meeting. They just made it before the doors of the meeting room were shut."

15

"LORD, IT IS GOOD FOR US TO BE HERE. IF YOU WANT, LET'S MAKE THREE TENTS"

CONTEXT

Since telling the parable of the Sower, Jesus has told many more parables, fed five thousand listeners, walked on water across the Sea of Galilee and been approached by the scribes and Pharisees with a hostile question. Possibly to get away from them for a break He has been for a prolonged trip northwest, to the coastal region of Tyre and Sidon, where He healed a Syro-Phoenician woman's daughter. On returning to Galilee, He has climbed a mountain, but has not escaped the crowds, who came to Him bringing with them the lame, blind, dumb and maimed for Him to heal them. As we saw regarding John the Baptist, this fulfilled what was expected of the Messiah, as recorded in Isaiah 35:5-6a. Then Jesus has fed four thousand people with seven loaves and a few fish, after which He has been approached again by the Pharisees and Sadducees wanting a sign, prompting Jesus to retreat north to Caesarea Philippi. While there He has asked the disciples who they thought He was. Peter has replied that He was the Christ. Immediately Jesus has begun preparing the disciples for what lay ahead, forewarning them that He was destined to suffer and be killed. Having been right about who Jesus was, Peter has now rebuked Him, saying that he was having none of it. Jesus has responded with a very sharp retort, implying that Peter's view of the situation was severely tempting. However, Jesus has not allowed Himself to be deflected and has proceeded to warn the disciples of what lay ahead for them also. They needed to listen, but one suspects that they did their best to put it out of their minds. Jesus must have felt very alone, misunderstood and unsupported. One wonders what He said to Father God that week. Father God had a stunning solution for keeping Jesus' mission on track and getting the ear of His disciples.

MATTHEW 17:1-13

QUESTIONS FOR THOUGHT OR DISCUSSION

What had happened six days before Jesus took Peter, James and John up the mountain with Him? (Matthew 16:13-20)

How had Peter responded to Jesus' prediction about His future? (Matthew 16:21-22)

How might Jesus have been feeling about Peter's response?

What do you think Jesus might have said to the Father?

"LORD ... IF YOU WANT, LET'S MAKE THREE TENTS"

What did the appearance of Moses and Elijah demonstrate?

How did Peter respond on the mountain?

What did Father God do and say and why?

What effect did seeing Jesus transfigured have on Peter's future responses to Jesus, when Jesus continued to warn His disciples about the way His life would end? (Matthew 20:17-19)

What information did Jesus add about His future on the way down the mountain?

What do we learn about the Father heart of God from Jesus' transfiguration?

COMMENTS

Jesus has climbed yet another mountain, taking only Peter, James and John with Him. Then He was transfigured and seen conversing with Moses and Elijah, representing the law and the prophets. Peter, James and John must have been awestruck. It was too much for Peter to watch in silence, but he did not know what to say. How could he have preferred the sound of his own voice to hearing what Jesus, Moses and Elijah had to say to each other? What a missed opportunity! Presumably he wanted to prolong the event, as he asked whether Jesus would like three booths for shelter. Even while he was speaking, a voice over-rode him telling the disciples to listen to Jesus, as He was the Father's beloved Son, in whom the Father was well pleased. This was not only a ratification of Peter's recognition of Jesus' identity, but also a wake-up call that however much they might not like what they would be hearing about Jesus' future from now on, they should pay attention to what He would be telling them. And in Peter's case, that he needed to learn to stop talking when he should be listening! Father God was desperate to get the disciples' attention onto

Jesus and when Jesus got talked over, He interrupted with a ratification of Jesus and a command that they were to listen to Him.

The disciples were terrified and fell flat on their faces, but Jesus came to them and touched them and told them to get up and not to fear. How gracious and gentle He was with them. When they opened their eyes there was Jesus standing alone, ready to set off down the mountain. Peter might have missed the conversation or part of it, but Father God had ensured that he had heard and seen what he really needed to hear and see, including that Moses and Elijah might have died, (or been taken up), but they were still living. The next time we read of Jesus forewarning the disciples that He would be betrayed and killed and on the third day be raised to life, it is no longer so fanciful, given the appearance of Moses and Elijah. We read of no more unhelpful responses from Peter, but instead silence. He was learning to listen.

MEDITATION

Your mind is racing as you climb yet another mountain with Jesus. This time you are going high and it is tough keeping up. Jesus seems subdued, serious, intent on really getting away from the crowds this time. You wonder why He is leading you to such a remote and inaccessible place. If He really is the Messiah, it is momentous that He has chosen you to be a close follower. It is now six days since Peter's declaration of recognition. But surely Jesus cannot really mean that He is heading for a violent death and that the price for you will be martyrdom too. It all seems so different from your previous assumptions. And scary.

> **17 After six days, Jesus took with him Peter, James, and John his brother, and brought them up into a high mountain by themselves. ² He was changed before them. His face shone like the sun, and his garments became as white as the light. ³ Behold, Moses and Elijah appeared to them talking with him.**

"LORD ... IF YOU WANT, LET'S MAKE THREE TENTS"

⁴ Peter answered and said to Jesus, "Lord, it is good for us to be here. If you want, let's make three tents here: one for you, one for Moses, and one for Elijah."

⁵ While he was still speaking, behold, a bright cloud overshadowed them. Behold, a voice came out of the cloud, saying, "This is my beloved Son, in whom I am well pleased. Listen to him."

⁶ When the disciples heard it, they fell on their faces, and were very afraid. ⁷ Jesus came and touched them and said, "Get up, and don't be afraid." ⁸ Lifting up their eyes, they saw no one, except Jesus alone.

⁹ As they were coming down from the mountain, Jesus commanded them, saying, "Don't tell anyone what you saw, until the Son of Man has risen from the dead."

¹⁰ His disciples asked him, saying, "Then why do the scribes say that Elijah must come first?"

¹¹ Jesus answered them, "Elijah indeed comes first, and will restore all things; ¹² but I tell you that Elijah has come already, and they didn't recognize him, but did to him whatever they wanted to. Even so the Son of Man will also suffer by them." ¹³ Then the disciples understood that he spoke to them of John the Baptizer.

OBSERVATIONS

Peter was so annoying, anything to shut him up! Father God did a good job of it!

For the three disciples present, this must have been a life changing moment. Their faith in Yahweh had been theoretical up until this point, witness the fact that they had not appealed to Him when they needed rescuing from the storm on the lake. Suddenly and possibly for the first time in their lives, they find themselves in the tangible presence of God.

They already knew that Jesus was no ordinary human being, as He could do things that nobody else could do, but recently Peter had declared that Jesus was the Messiah. It was no accident of timing that they now saw Jesus transfigured, so that His glory became visible, ratifying Peter's declaration. Hearing Yahweh speaking out of a cloud, further ratifying Jesus, was the kind of event that until that moment they had only heard about. No longer would it have been possible for them to see Jesus as no more than another human being. This event could only have changed their relationship with Him from one of respect to one of awe and potentially readiness to suffer. For probably the first time in their lives they had experienced the glory of God and they knew it.

16

"WHY WEREN'T WE ABLE TO CAST IT OUT?"

CONTEXT

The disciples that did not witness Jesus being transfigured were at the bottom of the mountain. It is interesting to speculate on why Jesus did not take all of the twelve up the mountain with Him. Maybe He wanted the nine to waylay the crowds, in order to be sure of not being interrupted by a crowd of people following Him up the mountain. Maybe the ones He left behind were not ready to see what Peter, James and John saw. Maybe Jesus was aware that He needed to be careful what He said in Judas' presence, lest He gave Judas cause to go to the authorities prematurely. Whatever the reason, the disciples found themselves put on the spot with a request for healing that they failed to meet.

MATTHEW 17:14-21

QUESTIONS FOR THOUGHT OR DISCUSSION

What was the father of the boy asking of the disciples and Jesus?

What do you think was causing the boy's illness?

Who do you think Jesus was most frustrated with when He asked how long He would have to endure His generation?

Why was Jesus so frustrated?

What did Jesus healing the boy say about Him and Father God?

What was wrong with the disciples' faith?

What possibilities for the disciples' faith did Jesus see?

COMMENTS

The disciples failed to heal the boy that had been brought to them, in spite of the fact that they had tried. When Jesus came down from the mountain, He rebuked a demon and the child was healed from that moment. Given that Jesus could do it, the disciples were left asking why they couldn't. Jesus' answer was their little faith. And in whom should their faith be placed? Obviously not in themselves, it wasn't normal for people to go around healing on the scale that Jesus did. That is why He was followed by such great crowds for so much of the time. Healing was an activity that required God's power. This is not the first time that Jesus has commented on the poverty of the disciples' faith. It seems a bit unfair on the disciples that they were upbraided for their lack of faith, when most of the rest of the world had even less faith. However, they were the ones getting to know Jesus and Jesus was keen for them to

"WHY WEREN'T WE ABLE TO CAST IT OUT?"

realize that their picture of Yahweh was inadequate. Jesus' comments on the level of faith that the disciples did not possess was about their not knowing Yahweh, or Father God and trusting in His power to act. If they had truly known Him as Creator of the world, they should not have had such difficulty believing in His ability to intervene in the present.

When first faced with the father of the child telling Him that His disciples had been unable to heal his son, Jesus bemoaned the faithlessness and perversity of His generation and wanted to know how long He would have to endure them. The author used to think that this had shades of condemnation in it, but she has come to see it as an expression of pain and grief over the obtuseness of the disciples, especially in the light of the contrast provided by the support that Jesus had just been receiving from Moses and Elijah. Perversity, sometimes translated corruption, is a strong term, defined in Collins Paperback Dictionary and Thesaurus (1996) as meaning "deliberately doing something different from what is thought normal or proper." Jesus is feeling the brunt of even His disciples' rebellion against Yahweh and therefore Himself. However, in the Greek, the word translated perverse is passive: "having been made perverse." This suggests the need to ask: "by whom?" It is not difficult to imagine that Jesus might have had the religious authorities and teachers in mind and that this was yet another reference to them and their failure to love God and teach the people to do the same. The people around Him were suffering the consequences.

If Jesus found being amongst unbelieving people a test of endurance, how must Father God feel about enduring history?! He must find failure to trust in His ability utterly insulting. Thankfully the faith that the father of the child had in Jesus' power to heal was not destroyed by the disciples' failure. Faced with the father's plea for mercy on his child, Jesus responded with immediate healing. We are left wondering what it was in the hearts of the disciples that was so out of tune with Yahweh? It did not take long for a number of possible explanations to surface, as we shall see in the days or weeks to come.

MEDITATION

The bottom of the mountain is in stark contrast to the top. There are numerous people pressing in and there is jostling, turmoil and tension. People are desperate for healing, especially one man in particular, pleading for his son, who has epilepsy. The disciples are desperate, they have all failed and Jesus has been nowhere to be seen. Will He ever reappear? And then, suddenly, He does.

> [14] When they came to the multitude, a man came to him, kneeling down to him and saying, [15] "Lord, have mercy on my son, for he is epileptic and suffers grievously; for he often falls into the fire, and often into the water. [16] So I brought him to your disciples, and they could not cure him."
>
> [17] Jesus answered, "Faithless and perverse generation! How long will I be with you? How long will I bear with you? Bring him here to me." [18] Jesus rebuked the demon, and it went out of him, and the boy was cured from that hour.
>
> [19] Then the disciples came to Jesus privately, and said, "Why weren't we able to cast it out?"
>
> [20] He said to them, "Because of your unbelief. For most certainly I tell you, if you have faith as a grain of mustard seed, you will tell this mountain, 'Move from here to there,' and it will move; and nothing will be impossible for you. [21] But this kind doesn't go out except by prayer and fasting."

OBSERVATIONS

I wonder what would happen if our little group agreed together to pray for a guy in church who used to be homeless and does not like living alone in his flat? What would it take for us to get to the point where we have real faith to expect deliverance from the fear that binds him?

17

"WHO THEN IS GREATEST IN THE KINGDOM OF HEAVEN?"

CONTEXT

The disciples were back home in Galilee after their trip north to Caesarea Philippi, where the Transfiguration took place. Jesus has again been talking about the fact that He is to be betrayed and killed and then raised to life. We read that the disciples were filled with grief. Then the tax collectors arrived. Neither Peter nor Jesus had the requisite money, but Jesus simply told Peter to go line fishing. When he did so, he found the very coin he needed for them both inside the mouth of the first fish that he caught, just as Jesus had told him that he would. He paid the tax.

The next thing we find is that the disciples were wondering about the Kingdom to which Jesus kept referring. They approached Jesus and asked Him: "Who then is greatest in the Kingdom of Heaven?"

How many of us dream of being notable, famous even? What is it we would like to be famous for? Is it about how we might benefit others, or about how we might get to look one better than others? If such thoughts are a part of us, then it is likely that we are out of line with Father God ourselves. He wants Jesus to have His rightful place as the One who is honoured, but even for God there was an ultimate price to pay on the cross for that to be possible.

The disciples were just like us and the rest of humanity. Despite all the amazing things that they had seen Jesus do, which they were unable to emulate, they were still hoping for a greatness of their own. They were aware that it might not look quite like they had imagined it in the past, but nevertheless they were still out for themselves. In this they were out of line with God and this might have been one of the reasons for which they were unable to heal the child whose father had come to them recently.

MATTHEW 18:1-9

QUESTIONS FOR THOUGHT OR DISCUSSION

Who do you think of as a great person?

Who did Jesus consider to be the greatest?

What are the characteristics of a child that Jesus was applauding?

What implications does Jesus' approval of childlike characteristics have for us?

How did Jesus view people who were indifferent to leading children astray?

"WHO THEN IS GREATEST IN THE KINGDOM OF HEAVEN?"

What was the attitude of Jesus to causes of sin?

Do you think the difference between a child and the disciples had anything to do with the inadequacy of their faith when it came to them being unable to heal the epileptic boy described in Matthew 17:14-21?

What does Jesus' response to the disciples tell us about Father God?

COMMENTS
The author's great person was the late Queen of the UK (Elizabeth ll). Jesus picked a child. That blows the author's mind.
What is it about being like a child that requires humility?

Becoming
In Jesus' day children had no status in society. They do not by and large spend time worrying about political issues; such issues are more likely to be lost on them. Their world is about their immediate needs and about exploring all that is new to them. Their sense of wonderment can be very endearing, as can their recourse to parental protection whenever they feel threatened. Part of getting to know their world involves getting to know their parents. What are the boundaries? How safe are they? What makes their parents smile? How can they become like them? Usually unconscious on the part of the child, but nevertheless their capacity to mimic is very real.

Father God loves it when our primary focus is on getting to know Him and becoming like Him. Children do not set out consciously to try to be like their parents, it happens sometimes in spite of their wishes. Their parents' nature is inbuilt via their DNA and then by spending time in their presence their habits rub off and they become like those whom they mimic.

This speaks of the importance to Jesus of us allowing the Holy Spirit to reign in our lives, as from Him comes our spiritual DNA. And when we mimic those we read about in the Bible and spend time with fellow believers and mimic those who remind us of God we allow Him to form His likeness in us.

The question is; are we most concerned with our character and how like Jesus we are? Or does it matter more to us that we have a respected role and recognized input and are thought to be great by those around us? Quite a challenge for some of us.

Trusting

Children in stable parts of the world are carefree. They do not need to worry about where the next meal is coming from, they rely totally on their parents for that and assume that all will be well. Not difficult if they have good parents and no reason to think otherwise. They are naturally trusting of their parents, unless they have been given reason to become otherwise.

This reflects the Sermon on the Mount, where Jesus talks about the lilies of the field being beautifully adorned, yet not doing anything to make it happen. The kind of trust that children display speaks of the certainty that we can have when we trust that God will provide for all our needs without our help and find the willingness not to be self-made and proud of it. This is about humility expressed in terms of dependency on God to provide for our needs.

Influencing

Children have no civic rights, they cannot vote, nor can they dictate to others. They are powerless to influence their social and economic circumstances, other than through depending on their parents. They are part of a unit and can only ask their parents to act on their behalf. The author can remember feeling similarly powerless at work and finding it difficult to be a Christian there, because it was not obvious to me how the Kingdom of God was being realized in a busy, provincial hospital. The staff were working for the benefit and wellbeing of sick people, but in human strength. There was virtually no room for the power of God to be made manifest. Praying for the sick was forbidden to staff and there was unbelief all around. What I did not do enough of was appealing to God behind the scenes to do something on behalf of my clients. I was a hospital social worker at the time and unconsciously did not believe that God was equal to the task of meeting the need all around me. I felt that I needed to try to make things happen on His behalf. However, when I did go into the chapel and ask Him very specifically to provide unusual answers for the needs of my clients, I saw Him do so in some amazing ways. We may not have any power, but we have a Father in heaven who has all the power in the universe, if only we remember that apart from Him, we can do nothing and to appeal to Him and believe in Him to intervene.

The question is: "Do we expect God to be at work in our world and our circumstances and do we make a habit of appealing to Him to act on our behalf and on the behalf of those around us, in our families, at work and at a national and international level?"

Identifying
The identity of a child is derived from their parents' name. If we call ourselves Christian, we are claiming allegiance to the One who is in the business of anointing His followers with the power of the Holy Spirit. The Holy Spirit was initially given on the anniversary of the giving of the law at Mount Sinai, not as a replacement for the law, but as the guarantee of power to love God and to keep His law and as the guarantor of our inheritance as God's children.

There is nothing here about position in society or in the church, nor is there anything about riches, power or influence. It is all about dependency on God and greatness derived from being in relationship with the greatest Being in the universe.

Jesus makes no bones about the fact that the opposite of humility, manifesting as concern for our own status, self-made independence, operating in our own strength and failing to identify with God; Father, Son and Holy Spirit is sin and if persisted in, will serve to ensure our self-chosen exclusion from the Kingdom of God. We cannot serve God and our own ends. Nor can we expect the Holy Spirit to flow through us with healing for others if we are not totally dependent on Him.

MEDITATION

Jesus and the disciples are alone together in a house in Capernaum. We can imagine they are very likely reclining around a table or the edges of a room, sharing a meal. Or maybe waiting for it to appear. It is a golden opportunity for the disciples to share with Jesus what is on their hearts and to ask Him about their concerns. Jesus has been talking to them about His impending death at the hands of the religious leaders, which they have not been expecting. Their current concern is about greatness and how status will play out in the Kingdom of Heaven.

> 18 In that hour the disciples came to Jesus, saying, "Who then is greatest in the Kingdom of Heaven?"
>
> ² Jesus called a little child to himself, and set him in the middle of them ³ and said, "Most certainly I tell you, unless you turn and become as little children, you will in no way enter into the Kingdom of Heaven. ⁴ Whoever therefore humbles himself as this little child is the greatest in the Kingdom of Heaven. ⁵ Whoever receives one such little child in my name receives me, ⁶ but whoever causes one of these little ones who believe in me to stumble, it would be better for him if a huge millstone were hung around his neck and that he were sunk in the depths of the sea.
>
> ⁷ "Woe to the world because of occasions of stumbling! For it must be that the occasions come, but woe to that person through whom the occasion comes! ⁸ If your hand or your foot causes you to stumble, cut it off and cast it from you. It is better for you to enter into life maimed or crippled, rather than having two hands or two feet to be cast into the eternal fire. ⁹ If your eye causes you

"WHO THEN IS GREATEST IN THE KINGDOM OF HEAVEN?"

to stumble, pluck it out and cast it from you. It is better for you to enter into life with one eye, rather than having two eyes to be cast into the Gehenna of fire.

OBSERVATIONS

The only way I can see of not minding being without status of any kind is to be obsessed with God and who He is and therefore able to forget self. It means finding satisfaction in simply being His child, not in achieving. It also means looking to Him alone for recognition, not to anyone else. It means death to self. It means taking up the cross and carrying it daily.

When we joined the scene, I saw a little girl, running from one disciple to another, folding her arms across their knees and looking up into their faces with an adorable smile. She was delightful, enough to warm the heart of anyone who saw her. All she needed to do was to be, nothing more. No achievement or status could ever add to her adorability. And that little girl represented me in the eyes of Jesus.

Then it occurred to me that she also represented Jesus and the way that He related to Daddy Abba Father God. In a manner closely related to the parables, Jesus was telling the disciples that He was the greatest, although so humbly and graciously that it was possible for them to miss it if they didn't listen carefully enough. He could just have said "I Am!" And given that Jesus and the Father were one and that no child is greater than their parent, then actually Jesus was talking about Yahweh, the great "I AM," who met with Moses in the desert all those centuries ago.

A picture of meteorites comes to mind, the miniature variety, small rocks hurtling through space in a group, close to the edge of the earth's atmosphere. They have taken their eyes off the sun for a moment to debate which of them is biggest.

18

"LORD, HOW OFTEN SHALL MY BROTHER SIN AGAINST ME, AND I FORGIVE HIM?"

CONTEXT

Jesus was still in Galilee and since His conversation with the disciples about who was the greatest, He has told them a couple of stories, one about the importance of looking for the lost sheep, illustrating the value of each little person and one about the importance of reconciliation with brothers or sisters who have wronged us. This did not involve the passive acceptance of wrongs, but rather the need to confront and reprove those who have wronged us in search of a response of repentance. Having heard this teaching, Peter came to Jesus to ask how many times he should forgive a brother or sister who had wronged him.

"LORD, HOW OFTEN SHALL MY BROTHER SIN AGAINST ME...?"

MATTHEW 18:21-35

QUESTIONS FOR THOUGHT OR DISCUSSION

What did Peter ask and what did Jesus say?

What are the implications of Jesus' story?

Are the implications eternal?

What does it mean to forgive?

Does forgiving include accepting ongoing abuse?

How can we forgive?

Do you know any present-day stories that help us with how to forgive?

Is forgiveness the same as reconciliation?

What does Jesus' story tell us about the Father heart of God?

COMMENTS

It costs to forgive. It means that we have to be willing to suffer loss on account of someone else's bankruptcy. This is not a very compelling idea until we remember our own bankruptcy. Which of us can claim to have honoured God and loved Him with all our heart, soul, strength and mind and to have loved our neighbour as ourselves one hundred per cent? How can we ever make it up to God for our own failings in this regard? Any failure to love God amounts to a slight against Him. Not only that, but God also takes personally how we treat others: "because you did it to one of the least of these my brothers, you did it to me." (Matthew 25:40b).

Ultimately the opposite of loving someone is seeking their annihilation. We see this made bare when the human race attempted to annihilate Jesus through crucifixion. We also see God's mercy shown through Jesus' words from the cross: "Father, forgive them, for they don't know what they are doing." (Luke 23:34). The price God pays not to annihilate us is to accept our would-be annihilation of Him, the ultimate insult possible to the Creator of all things. If God is willing to pay the ultimate price on the cross to restore us into relationship with Himself, who are we to refuse to be reconciled with others, mostly at a much lower cost to ourselves than God has suffered for us? And if we do refuse, there will be consequences, designed as a wake-up call to bring us back to our senses. We cannot have one rule for ourselves and another for everyone else. If we want to be forgiven, we have to live forgivingly ourselves, however challenging we find it, as many of us do.

The author likes the story that Corrie ten Boom told of meeting the prison camp guard who was responsible for her sister's death when they were prisoners of war. He was present at a talk that Corrie gave after the war was over and he went forward to thank her. Corrie recognized him and everything in her recoiled from shaking his outstretched hand. She sent an arrow prayer to God asking for His forgiveness to flow through her to the guard and as she did so, she was filled with compassion for him and enabled to shake his hand.[2]

Tearing up someone's account when they owe us does not mean that we have to subject ourselves to continuing abuse. It does mean that we are to be ready to receive anyone who has given us cause for offence if they come to us to say sorry. We are not told to wait for that moment before we forgive them.

Maybe the issue of unforgiveness was another reason for the disciples' inability to heal the child that had been brought to them while Jesus was up the mountain being transfigured.

MEDITATION

Jesus and the disciples are still in Capernaum, or certainly in Galilee. It seems that since their return from Caesarea Philippi they have managed to escape the notice of the crowds and Jesus is preparing the disciples for what lies ahead. This involves more teaching and more stories, including on the subject of forgiveness and reconciliation.

Forgiveness does not simply mean tearing up someone's account if it's in debt. Jesus has just been telling the disciples that they are to seek out any brother or sister who has wronged them and to point out their fault, with a view to them acknowledging it and changing their ways. This was about seeking reconciliation in a spirit of forgiveness, not of revenge.

[21] Then Peter came and said to him, "Lord, how often shall my brother sin against me, and I forgive him? Until seven times?"

[22] Jesus said to him, "I don't tell you until seven times, but, until seventy times seven. [23] Therefore the Kingdom of Heaven is like a certain king, who wanted to settle accounts with his servants. [24] When he had begun to settle, one was brought to him who owed him ten thousand talents. [25] But because he couldn't pay, his lord commanded him to be sold, with his wife, his children, and all that he had, and payment to be made. [26] The servant therefore fell down and knelt before him, saying, 'Lord, have patience with me, and I will repay you all!' [27] The lord of that servant, being moved with compassion, released him and forgave him the debt.

[28] "But that servant went out and found one of his fellow servants who owed him one hundred denarii, and he grabbed him and took him by the throat, saying, 'Pay me what you owe!'

[29] "So his fellow servant fell down at his feet and begged him, saying, 'Have patience with me, and I will repay you!' [30] He would not, but went and cast him into prison until he should pay back that which was due. [31] So when his fellow servants saw what was done, they were

exceedingly sorry, and came and told their lord all that was done. ³² Then his lord called him in and said to him, 'You wicked servant! I forgave you all that debt because you begged me. ³³ Shouldn't you also have had mercy on your fellow servant, even as I had mercy on you?' ³⁴ His lord was angry, and delivered him to the tormentors until he should pay all that was due to him. ³⁵ So my heavenly Father will also do to you, if you don't each forgive your brother from your hearts for his misdeeds."

OBSERVATIONS

I have often wondered whether the picture of the first servant going to jail and suffering torture relates to before death or after death. On reflection, that servant was never going to be able to pay off his debt, so the imprisonment and torture were likely to be ongoing. This makes me think that the fate of the first servant was an eternal one, relating to after death. It reinforces what Jesus had to say about those who disobeyed God without repenting, that "Not everyone who calls Me 'Lord, Lord' will enter the Kingdom of Heaven."

19

"COMMAND THAT THESE, MY TWO SONS, MAY SIT, ONE ON YOUR RIGHT HAND AND ONE ON YOUR LEFT HAND, IN YOUR KINGDOM."

CONTEXT

After Jesus had answered Peter's question about forgiveness, He left Galilee and went into Judea, east of the Jordan. Word got around, large crowds followed Him and He healed those who came to Him. The Pharisees also came, to test Him with their questions on divorce. Some little children were brought to Him, only for the disciples to rebuke those who brought them. The disciples apparently had not taken in Jesus' earlier teaching on the status of little children, but Jesus remained consistent in saying not to hinder them, and He laid hands on them, reinforcing His teaching that the Kingdom of Heaven belongs to such as them.

Then a rich young ruler approached Jesus and Jesus responded to him by telling him to sell all that he had. The man went away sad, prompting Jesus to comment that it is easier for a camel to pass through the eye of a needle than for a rich man to enter the Kingdom of Heaven. Peter wanted to know what the disciples were going to get for giving up everything to follow Jesus. Jesus responded: "Most certainly I tell you that you who have followed me, in the regeneration when the Son of Man will sit on the throne of his glory, you also will sit on twelve thrones, judging the twelve tribes of Israel." (Matthew 19:28).

Not long after that Jesus set off for Jerusalem and on the way, He took the twelve aside and told them that He was going to be crucified and raised to life again on the third day.

MATTHEW 20:20-28

QUESTIONS FOR THOUGHT OR DISCUSSION

Who was Jesus?

Who is on Jesus' left hand in heaven? (Psalm 110:1, Matthew 22:41-45, Hebrews 10:11-14)

Given your answers to the previous two questions, what might Jesus have said to James and John?

What did Jesus say to James and John?

Why did Jesus respond the way He did?

What might Jesus have felt when James and John insisted that they could share His cup?

How did Jesus' affirmation that James and John would indeed drink from His bitter cup play out in their lives? (Acts 12:1-2, Rev 1:9)

Do you think that James' and John's mother would have made her request had she realized the implications of what she was asking for?

Think of someone who lives like a servant. How do you rate them? Do you think of them as great? Is it your aspiration to be like them?

What does Jesus' response to James and John tell us about Father God?

COMMENTS

It was not long after Jesus' teaching on forgiveness that James and John caused upset among the other ten disciples. They went with their mother to ask Jesus for the pre-eminent positions in His Kingdom. Jesus did not simply dismiss them as out of order. He responded, as He so often did when put on the spot, with a question of His own: "Are you able to drink the cup that I am about to drink, and be baptized with the baptism that I am baptized with?" Whilst ever the world is in rebellion against God, there is a price to pay for being close to Jesus. The world is reined against Him and sooner or later our loyalty to Him will bring the same kind of hostility down on us. The disciples had no idea of the price that Jesus was about to pay for God's kingdom to be established and no-one could expect to join Him by any other route.

James and John protested that they were able and willing to pay the price, little realizing what they were saying. Their protest of loyalty must have warmed Jesus' heart and He responded by accepting their protestation: "You will indeed drink my cup, and be baptized with the baptism that I am baptized with." And drink it they did. James was one of the earliest Christian martyrs, killed by the sword for his loyalty to Jesus after Jesus' resurrection. John ended up exiled to Patmos, again because the authorities wanted to silence his witness to Jesus. Wanting prominence in God's Kingdom is nothing short of dangerous from a worldly point of view! Jesus was right that James and John's mother did not know what she was asking. It was not only a dangerous request; it was also a futile one and indicated that they still did not recognize the implications of who Jesus was. He must have been aware that the place at the Father's right hand was His by right, but He did not say so. He just said that it was in the Father's gift, not His own to grant what they were asking. His self-effacement stands in stark contrast to the behaviour of James and John and not only them but also the other disciples, who were affronted. Here was an opportunity to forgive, but in fact they were all harbouring similar hopes for themselves. Jesus took the opportunity to paint a different option for them, that they should become like servants of one another, or even slaves, if they wanted to be great in His eyes, on the basis that He was among them as a servant Himself.

MEDITATION

You are on yet another journey with Jesus, which in practice means another long walk. The road is dusty and strewn with stones. Because Jesus is there, lots of other people are milling around, following Him. You have left the Jordan behind and are on the long climb out of the rift valley, up towards Jericho and then Jerusalem. Not long before, Jesus has taken you aside, along with the other disciples, to talk yet again about being crucified. You are sad and dread Him being right. You don't understand how it fits with the idea that you will be judging the twelve tribes of Israel in Jesus' Kingdom.

> [20] Then the mother of the sons of Zebedee came to him with her sons, kneeling and asking a certain thing of him. [21] He said to her, "What do you want?"
>
> She said to him, "Command that these, my two sons, may sit, one on your right hand and one on your left hand, in your Kingdom."

²² But Jesus answered, "You don't know what you are asking. Are you able to drink the cup that I am about to drink, and be baptized with the baptism that I am baptized with?"

They said to him, "We are able."

²³ He said to them, "You will indeed drink my cup, and be baptized with the baptism that I am baptized with; but to sit on my right hand and on my left hand is not mine to give, but it is for whom it has been prepared by my Father."

²⁴ When the ten heard it, they were indignant with the two brothers.

²⁵ But Jesus summoned them, and said, "You know that the rulers of the nations lord it over them, and their great ones exercise authority over them. ²⁶ It shall not be so among you; but whoever desires to become great among you shall be your servant. ²⁷ Whoever desires to be first among you shall be your bondservant, ²⁸ even as the Son of Man came not to be served, but to serve, and to give his life as a ransom for many."

OBSERVATIONS

Leading by serving is definitely a counter-cultural idea. It requires an eye only for what Jesus thinks of us, not what anybody else thinks.

20

"LORD, DON'T YOU CARE THAT MY SISTER LEFT ME TO SERVE ALONE? ASK HER THEREFORE TO HELP ME."

CONTEXT

Jesus was on His way up to Jerusalem with His disciples. He had sent seventy-two people ahead of Him to heal the sick in the villages along His route and to proclaim that the Kingdom of God had come near. He had told them not to stay in any town where they were not welcomed and had pronounced woes on Chorazin, Bethsaida and Capernaum before turning to the Father to praise Him for revealing the things of the Kingdom to little children. We considered that event in the section on Jesus' own prayer life. Not long afterwards an expert in the law approached Jesus to ask what he must do to inherit eternal life. Jesus

"LORD, DON'T YOU CARE THAT MY SISTER LEFT ME TO SERVE ALONE?"

responded by telling the parable of the Good Samaritan. Then Jesus and the disciples reached Bethany, although Luke does not name the village.

LUKE 10:38-42

QUESTIONS FOR THOUGHT OR DISCUSSION

What did the appearance of Jesus and twelve of His friends mean for Mary and Martha?

What did Mary do about it?

Might you have expected the disciples to say something about Mary's behaviour?

What did Martha do?

How was Martha feeling about Mary?

Why did Martha object to Mary's behaviour?

What did Martha say to Jesus?

How did Jesus view the behaviour of each of the sisters?

How did Jesus respond to Martha?

Do you think the disciples would have been surprised by what Jesus had to say to Martha?

What does Jesus' response to Martha's request tell us about the Father's heart for answering prayer?

COMMENTS

Martha set to work to feed their thirteen, very likely unexpected, guests. Meanwhile Mary sat down at Jesus' feet to listen to what He had to say. Mary's behaviour was utterly counter-cultural. She was in with the men, not something that was expected of a woman. It is interesting that there is no record that any of Jesus' disciples expressed disapproval, whatever they might have been thinking to themselves. Maybe by this time they had learned better of it and begun to assimilate the alternative approach to life that Jesus was teaching them to adopt. After all, they had been rebuked by Jesus for turning children away and for criticizing a stranger for praying for people in Jesus' name. This time they held their peace.

Interestingly the objection to Mary's unconventional behaviour came not from any of the men but from another woman, her sister Martha. She clearly thought that Mary's place was in the kitchen, pulling her weight to prepare the meal for everyone and she was pretty annoyed at Mary's absence from her duty. She became sufficiently frustrated and angry to interrupt Jesus and appeal to Him to send Mary to help her. Jesus refused her request. In doing so He extended enormous graciousness and acceptance to Mary, way beyond societal norms for the treatment of women. It is easy to imagine that the disciples were glad that they had kept their mouths shut! Jesus clearly understood and appreciated Mary's love for Him and did not want to despise her compliment and by implication Mary herself. Instead, He fed back to Martha what He saw in her.

When the author imagines herself in Martha's shoes, her reflex reaction is to take exception with Jesus for what He said. What did He want and what was I supposed to do about it? Sit down with Mary and the men and leave the meal for later? Daylight was not going to last forever. Enrol the men in the kitchen to get the meal faster later on? There would not be room and they would not know what to do, even were they willing. An unlikely prospect. Then I started to reflect. Maybe Jesus has a point, something simpler would be just as good, there is no need to go to great lengths just to impress. If I was angry and annoyed,

"LORD, DON'T YOU CARE THAT MY SISTER LEFT ME TO SERVE ALONE?"

does that square with loving my neighbour as myself? Since when was it my place to make Mary's decisions for her about how she spent her time? That amounted to control, never a loving way to treat someone. So hard to get it right!! And what did Jesus mean by the good part? Maybe He would not have minded going hungry if it meant that He had my attention. Or maybe it was a recognition that the role prescribed for women was not an enviable one. Such empathy and so much more compassionate than any other man I have ever known. Jesus loves me too much to allow anything in my heart that displeases Him to go unchallenged.

MEDITATION

Bethany. Imagine a sleepy village about two miles from Jerusalem, over the brow of the hill and out of sight. A world away. No hustle and bustle in the streets. No frequent influxes of festival crowds. Only occasional sight of Roman soldiers charged with keeping the peace. No marketplace. A handful of houses. Neighbours who know each other. A subsistence existence, picking and preserving fruit, weaving rugs to sell in order to buy what cannot be produced for themselves. Day to day, hand to mouth, precarious existence.

We do not know how Jesus came to visit Mary and Martha. They may have been related to Jesus in some way. In Bethany they were well placed on the route up to Jerusalem for any traveller to drop in for a meal. We also do not know whether they had any warning of Jesus' imminent arrival. It is very possible that they did not, but either way the near Eastern culture of hospitality made it unthinkable not to feed their guests. Jesus did not travel alone, so suddenly Mary and Martha are faced with feeding at least fifteen instead of two!

> [38] As they went on their way, he entered into a certain village, and a certain woman named Martha received him into her house. [39] She had a sister called Mary, who also sat at Jesus' feet, and heard his word. [40] But Martha was distracted with much serving, and she

came up to him, and said, "Lord, don't you care that my sister left me to serve alone? Ask her therefore to help me."

⁴¹ Jesus answered her, "Martha, Martha, you are anxious and troubled about many things, ⁴² but one thing is needed. Mary has chosen the good part, which will not be taken away from her."

OBSERVATIONS

Only one thing is needed, to be focussed on Jesus and attentive to His perspective and will. Nothing else needs to bother us. That is a bit of a challenge!

21

"HOW DID THE FIG TREE IMMEDIATELY WITHER AWAY?"

CONTEXT

Jesus has reached Jerusalem. In Matthew's account, Jesus cursed the fig tree the morning after He had caused a disturbance in the Temple by throwing the tables of the moneychangers over and the seats of those selling doves. The sale of the birds and animals in the Temple was a service for those who had travelled long distances in order to offer a sacrifice. It was much easier for people to do their shopping on arrival than to travel bringing their sacrifice with them. A sacrifice had to be without defect (Leviticus 1:3) and there was real risk of their animals being maimed or killed en-route. It was far better to bring the money instead and to buy an animal or bird on arrival. There was nothing wrong with that. The Temple had its own currency, so the moneychangers were there to make the Temple currency available and as it was their livelihood, they might be expected to make a profit. There was nothing wrong with that either. Jesus was angry that the Temple had become a brigands' lair. Brigand doesn't mean thief; it means would-be violent revolutionary. The priests and leaders of the Temple had become aligned with a desire to see the Kingdom of God brought in by force. Jesus was utterly opposed to this.[3] Ironic that the religious leaders were so afraid of Jesus upsetting Rome.

Not only that, but Jesus was also putting Himself in the place of the Temple. By disrupting the moneychangers and sellers of doves, He prevented, for however short a period of time, the Temple sacrifices from taking place. Meanwhile He healed blind and lame people who sought Him out in the Temple. This was revolutionary in a different way. Jesus was suggesting that coming to Him was more effective than offering a sacrifice according to the Temple rituals. Normally the blind and lame were not even allowed into the Temple, following on from David forbidding them access to his palace (2 Samuel 5:6-10). When David took Jerusalem, the Jebusites were so sure of the fortress's impregnability that they had taunted David that only the blind and lame were on duty. David did not want to be reminded of the insult. Jesus was challenging this and turning it upside down.[4] Little wonder that the high priest had designs to silence Him.

MATTHEW 21:18-22

QUESTIONS FOR THOUGHT OR DISCUSSION

How did Jesus respond when He was tempted to turn stones into bread after forty days of fasting in the wilderness? (Matthew 4:4)

"HOW DID THE FIG TREE IMMEDIATELY WITHER AWAY?"

What preceded the cursing of the fig tree in Jesus' life?

What struck the disciples when Jesus cursed the fig tree?

What did the withered fig tree represent?

What did the mountain that Jesus referred to signify?

What future use would the Temple have after Jesus' death?

What was Jesus communicating to the disciples and why in such graphic fashion? (Matthew 23:37-39 and 1 Kings 9:1-9)

What did Jesus have to say in answer to the disciples' question?

How and when did what Jesus was signifying play out in Israel's national life?

What does this tell us about the Father heart of God for answering prayer?

What would have characterized a national life pleasing to Jesus in His day?

How would Jesus view contemporary national life wherever you are living?

What needs to change for your national life to be pleasing to Jesus?

Do you believe that your prayers can bring such a transformation about?

What do Jesus' actions and words tell us about Father God?

COMMENTS

It is easy to miss why Jesus cursed the fig tree. Matthew tells us that Jesus went to inspect it because He was hungry and hoped to find some figs that He could eat. It could be seen as a reaction of pique on Jesus' part but for the fact that that does not fit with His behaviour and attitude at other times, for example in the wilderness. There He was really hungry after forty days of fasting and what is more nobody, but Father God and the angels and demons, was watching. Even when sorely tempted to do so, Jesus refused to use His power to meet His own physical need. Unlikely then that He would have 'lost it' over a fig tree. So what was Jesus really thinking about and why did He do anything as destructive?

Jesus was consumed with longing for fellowship with the people of Jerusalem and recognition by them and was instead finding it necessary to challenge them to turn back to God. Nowhere was this so poignant than in the Temple, where He rightly could expect to find those who would love Him the most. Instead He found Himself at odds with them. Had they truly loved God they would also have recognized and loved Him. The fact that they did not held serious consequences both for them personally and for the Temple and Jerusalem. The shrivelled fig tree was a symbol of impending destruction. The disciples did not understand it at the time, but they did remember it. At the time they expressed amazement that it should wither so quickly and completely in response to nothing more than a word from Jesus. Jesus took the opportunity to link the visual aid of the withered fig tree to the Temple, which He referred to as "this mountain," and to comment on the power of prayer to effect its eventual destruction. The disciples must have been encouraged to remember this incident when, after Jesus' death and resurrection, they were facing persecution themselves at the hands of the Temple authorities. It was only a matter of a few decades after Jesus' death and resurrection that Jerusalem was sacked and the whole Temple edifice razed to the ground by the Romans.

The withered fig tree did not reflect anything individualistic. Jesus was depicting the impending doom of a nation and their way of life, using the fig tree as a visual image. So, we need to ask ourselves: "Are there mountains equivalent to the Israelite Temple of Jesus' day in our own society?" Put another way, what is there about our contemporary national life that would upset Jesus?

Maybe it would help to imagine a society in which the national culture would be a delight in Jesus' view. There would be no child sacrifice on high places. Think no abortion. Marriage would be between one man and one woman for life. There would be no partnerships and definitely no one-night stands. First intercourse involves the shedding of blood and signifies a life-long covenant. When God made His covenant with Abraham, recorded for us in Genesis 15, Abraham divided the animals and laid them in two lines, ready to pass between them. That would have signified that he would remain loyal to Yahweh, in return for protection against any attacker, or expect the same fate that the animals had suffered, should he rebel. However, instead of Abraham being required to pass between the lines of animals, Abraham saw a flaming pot doing so. God was saying: "If you default, I will be the One to bear the consequences on your behalf." Later St Paul wrote about husbands loving their wives as Jesus loves the church. Only the Holy Spirit can enable us to love one another this sacrificially and Jesus' death and resurrection reminds us that there is always hope for mercy. But the message is that there are consequences for entering into a covenant and then breaking it.

The laws and ordinances laid down for Israel in the Old Testament were designed to ensure a just and egalitarian society. In such a society today, there would be no need for food banks or homelessness. Economic units would be family groupings, not individuals. There would also be fair-pay and honesty would be taken for granted. Government statistics would give a true picture of what is happening on the ground and the Government would be aware of any gaps in provision by the State.

We each have daily choices to make, either to behave in ways that reflect God's standards or in ways that do not. At work the time came when the author was expected to tick a box on completed forms about clients to say that they had been given the paperwork within a month of their assessment. However, this was an administrative task that was routinely failing to happen, so I declined to tick the relevant boxes. I am not sure what would have happened when my statistics were reviewed at the end of that year as I changed jobs before the situation came to a head. What I am clear about is that skewed statistics do nothing to help the disadvantaged people to whom they refer; they simply save the skins of the responsible intermediate managers. I cannot imagine Jesus being indifferent to such a culture.

I used to feel powerless to effect change, but now I think that if I take responsibility for behaving righteously whenever a choice to do so or not to do so has to be made, the results of such choices have the potential to mount up. Every wave is composed of millions of individual molecules of water and if enough of them are going in the same direction the wave grows until it breaks and the tide comes in. Conversely, every unrighteous or dishonest action on our parts, however seemingly small or insignificant, constitutes the equivalent of another shrivelled leaf on the fig tree. The choice is ours to make.

MEDITATION

Yesterday you were in the Temple with Jesus and He caused quite a stir, overturning the tables of the money changers and the benches of those selling doves. He was so full of indignation and righteous zeal that you decided to keep your distance. Jesus' actions would surely inflame the authorities and they are already out to kill Him. You wish that He would be a bit more circumspect. The next thing you knew, Jesus was healing blind and lame people, who were coming to Him in the Temple with no rebuke from Him. When is Jesus going to stop turning the world upside down? He must have been aware that such people were not allowed in the Temple precincts.

Then came the walk to Bethany, to spend the night in the house of Mary and Martha, but you haven't slept at all well as there is so much going round in your mind. You have a sense of foreboding, but you cannot put your finger on the reason. Jesus is keen to get back to Jerusalem and you have set out early with Him. Scared and confused as you are, you do not want to intrude on Mary and Martha's hospitality plus Jesus seems to be on a mission and you do not want to be left out.

> [18] Now in the morning, as he returned to the city, he was hungry. [19] Seeing a fig tree by the road, he came to it and found nothing on it but leaves. He said to it, "Let there be no fruit from you forever!"
>
> Immediately the fig tree withered away.
>
> [20] When the disciples saw it, they marveled, saying, "How did the fig tree immediately wither away?"
>
> [21] Jesus answered them, "Most certainly I tell you, if you have faith and don't doubt, you will not only do what was done to the fig tree, but even if you told this mountain, 'Be taken up and cast into the sea,' it would be done. [22] All things, whatever you ask in prayer, believing, you will receive."

OBSERVATIONS

Sometimes it is tempting to think that judgment seems a long time coming. The speed with which the fig tree withered is a salutary reminder that judgment is not only certain, but that it will also be swift and total when the time comes. Not something to be longed for at all.

22

"WHY THIS WASTE?"

CONTEXT

Passover was drawing ever closer. Since cursing the fig tree on the way from Bethany to Jerusalem, Jesus has spent a great many hours in the Temple, teaching the people. The Pharisees were furious with Him for turning over the tables of the money changers and were asking Jesus questions and demanding to know where His authority came from. Jesus responded with parables about two sons, tenant farmers and a wedding banquet, all told at the Pharisees' expense. The Pharisees were becoming desperate to trap Jesus through what He said and both they and the Sadducees were interrupting Jesus' teaching with questions,

"WHY THIS WASTE?"

about paying taxes, the resurrection and the greatest commandment. Jesus turned the tables onto His questioners and asked in turn who they thought the Son of Man was. They were unwilling to answer Him and finally stopped coming with their questions. This left Jesus free to get on with teaching the people and He wasted no time in commenting on how He viewed the Pharisees, to the crowds and to the disciples.

Then He left the Temple and sat down on the Mount of Olives. This afforded the disciples the opportunity to ask Jesus questions of their own, leading to a conversation about the end of the age and more parables, this time about ten virgins, talents and sheep and goats. Then they returned to Bethany.

MATTHEW 26:6-13

QUESTIONS FOR THOUGHT OR DISCUSSION

What did the woman's gesture signify?

How did the disciples respond?

What might the disciples have had in mind? (See Matthew 19:21 for example)

How did Jesus respond to the disciples?

How did Jesus respond to the woman?

What did the disciples' response say about their attitude to Jesus?

Did the disciples' response affect Jesus' commitment to them?

How did the woman differ from the disciples?

What do Jesus' responses to the woman and to the disciples tell us about Father God?

COMMENTS
Maybe Jewish culture two thousand years ago was in some ways not so very different from our own (in the UK). The disciples' reaction to the woman's extravagant gesture was far more economically focussed than people focussed. But they could not say that they could have done with the money if the woman did not need it, so they dressed it up as concern for the poor. Or maybe they were genuinely concerned for the poor and mindful of Jesus' response to the rich, young man that he should sell what he owned and give the proceeds to the poor. Either way they unwittingly detracted from Jesus and any worth He might be considered to have. If that was all that His best friends could muster, how must it have hurt Him to live among us? I imagine it hurts Him still. The woman, by contrast, must have warmed Jesus' heart. Her gesture was outrageous, generous, extravagant, irreversible. The perfume was worth a lifetime's savings, a year's income, a buffer against possible future destitution. She could not rethink and have it back. Her action represented adoration, love, total commitment, maybe gratitude, giving of everything of value she had ever owned. And certainty that Jesus would receive it. You would not waste everything on someone who might reject it (and you) when it was too late to reseal the jar.

Jesus upbraided His disciples for their negative response and defended the woman. He could have upbraided the disciples for their disregard for Himself, but He chose not to do that. Instead, He offered the woman His support, as well as His gratitude. Then He took the opportunity to offer yet another word of warning regarding what was coming, that He would not be with them for much longer, aimed at fortifying the disciples to weather the storm when it came. Such a preparation for burial must have been priceless for Jesus. Instead of the stench of blood, sweat, tears and human excrement for the hours that it would take to die, He took with Him to the cross a perfume in His hair that would mitigate against all the other smells intrinsic to crucifixion. Not to mention the psychological impact of such generous love. The disciples still had a lot to learn and Matthew makes no bones about recording the fact. Yet Jesus' love for and commitment to them remained undiminished.

MEDITATION

It has been a long day. There is an urgency about Jesus' teaching now and He keeps referring to the fact that He expects to be crucified imminently. You do not want to believe Him. You prefer to focus on the strangeness of the fig tree withering, the increasing crowds arriving in Jerusalem for the festival, the number of stories that you have heard Jesus tell since this morning. But you have to admit that the animosity of the religious leaders is very worrying and so is the fact that Jesus has made no attempt to pacify them. You do not understand Him at all. In fact, you are glad to be back in the relative safety of Bethany. Now you can relax for a while.

But even here, the unexpected does not stop happening.

> [6] Now when Jesus was in Bethany, in the house of Simon the leper, [7] a woman came to him having an alabaster jar of very expensive ointment, and she poured it on his head as he sat at the table. [8] But when his disciples saw this, they were indignant, saying, "Why this waste? [9] For this ointment might have been sold for much and given to the poor."
>
> [10] However, knowing this, Jesus said to them, "Why do you trouble the woman? She has done a good work for me. [11] For you always have the poor with you, but you don't always have me. [12] For in pouring this ointment on my body, she did it to prepare me for burial. [13] Most certainly I tell you, wherever this Good News is preached in the whole world, what this woman has done will also be spoken of as a memorial of her."

OBSERVATIONS

It is comforting to think that the disciples could be so unwittingly insensitive towards Jesus and yet they were His instruments for making known the meaning of the crucifixion and resurrection and who Jesus really was. Jesus took no offence at their disregard for Him, He remained steadfastly other centred in His concern for the woman's feelings and for the disciples' need to be prepared for what lay just around the corner.

PART 4

JESUS AND THE SICK AND NEEDY

23

A LEPER AND A ROMAN CENTURION

CONTEXT

Matthew devoted three chapters of his Gospel to the Sermon on the Mount, recording teaching by Jesus encompassing a wide range of topics. It is quite possible that Jesus was speaking in a natural amphitheatre and either way we are told that a large crowd had followed Him up the mountain to listen to Him. As Jesus came down from the mountain, heading for Capernaum, large crowds followed Him and a leper approached Him.

MATTHEW 8:1-13

QUESTIONS FOR THOUGHT OR DISCUSSION

What was life like for lepers in the time of Jesus?

What might have prevented the leper from reaching Jesus?

How did Jesus' response to the leper differ from that of other people?

Why did Jesus tell the leper to go and show himself to the priest?

How would most Jews have viewed the centurion?

How did Jesus view the centurion?

What risks was Jesus taking in responding to the centurion?

What is the normal attitude of occupying forces to subject people?

How did the centurion differ from most other officers of the Roman army?

Why was Jesus surprised by the centurion?

Was it surprising that Jesus healed the centurion's servant? Why, or why not?

What do we learn about Father God from looking at Jesus?

COMMENTS

This leper stands out. As a contagious person, he was banished to the outskirts of society and would not be expected to be in amongst a large crowd of people. He must have been pretty determined to reach Jesus if he was prepared to run the gauntlet of the crowd's horrified and disapproving looks and their retreat from his presence. That very retreat would have been the one consolation, in that it would have given him a clear path into Jesus' presence, who alone did not shun being close to him. Not only was the leper a determined character, he must also have had absolute faith in Jesus' ability to heal him or he would not have taken the risk involved in trying to reach Him. Even with faith like that he did not presume on Jesus' will, he simply stated what he believed Him to be capable of. The author imagines that Jesus was thrilled to see someone with such trust in Him and that that drew out of Him a desire to respond in such a way as to ratify the man's faith. He was indeed capable of healing leprosy and He proceeded to do so in spite of it being incurable. The result was immediately obvious and Jesus sent the man away to the priest to present the offering commanded by Moses for the ratification of his healing. Some translations of the Bible imply that this was so that other people would have grounds to believe that he was healed and to allow him to mix in society again without needing to protect themselves from him for fear of becoming infected themselves. However, a literal translation suggests that he was to go to the priest for a testimony to them, meaning the priests. The people present could see that he was healed, it was the priests who needed confronting with the reality of Jesus' power. They would have known that the man had been a leper and would have had no excuse for not believing what they saw. Nor would they have had any case against Jesus for encouraging anyone to break the law by bypassing the cleansing and ratification ceremonies, recorded in Leviticus 14:1-9. Their refusal to believe was a choice, as is still the case for some religious leaders today. Maybe it was because with power comes the temptation to control and the ability to control creates an illusion of safety. Jesus was not controllable and flouted all the normal allegiances expected in order not to rock the boat.

Eventually Jesus reached Capernaum, the town in which He was living. The Roman centurion would have been another ostracized figure, seen much as the German army officers were seen in Jersey during World War Two for example; the representatives of a hated occupying force. Jesus never responded to people on the basis of categorization, however, He always saw beyond such labels to the heart of the person standing before Him. This would have taken courage, as being kind to a centurion was not designed to endear Him to any Jew, powerful and powerless alike. The fact that the centurion approached Jesus in front of a huge crowd of people, who would have been following Him down off the mountain, did not deter Jesus. He only had one allegiance and that was to the Father and His will to bless all people. He did not hesitate, He offered to go to the centurion's house to heal his servant. The author is reminded of doctors who risk their lives when they treat enemy militia in hospital during times of armed conflict. Jesus' courage knew no bounds. Moreover, bearing in mind the normal mindset of occupying forces towards their subjects, the centurion's response should strike us as surprising. He tells Jesus that he, the centurion, is not worthy to have Jesus under his roof. Then he goes on to say: "For I am also a man under authority." In saying this he implies recognition of the divine and powerful authority under which Jesus was operating and not only that, but that it was an authority that surpassed that of Rome. It was an astonishing admission and one that was not lost on Jesus. Jesus Himself was amazed and said as much for the benefit of those who were within earshot. He also took the opportunity to make clear that such faith was the passport into His Kingdom and that without it the Jews would miss their inheritance. Claiming Abraham as their ancestor was not enough, only those with faith in Jesus would be joining Abraham's family. This amounted to an implied claim of Messiahship on Jesus' part. Then He healed the centurion's servant by remote, simply through the power of His spoken word.

MEDITATION

It can't be true. I must be seeing things. If I get a good night's sleep, it will hopefully be gone in the morning. If not, maybe I could pretend

I hadn't noticed it. But what if it is true? If I ignore it, I'll be putting the rest of my family at risk of catching it from me. I can't believe this. If the only way to protect them is to leave, my life is over, yet I'm not dead. I wish I were, I might as well be. I'll have to join the leper colony to survive, outside the city walls. No more time with my family, or my wife. No more communal meals. No more work - how will my family survive? What will happen to my children?

How am I going to live? It will be cold at night with no roof over my head and searing hot by day with no roof for shade. There will be no protection from wild animals, they won't know I've got leprosy and they shouldn't come near. This is a nightmare. And nothing to look forward to but the disappearance of my fingers and toes, so that I won't be able to eat or walk. Blank despair. I only hope my family will bring me food to make up for my not having any money and not being able to go to the market anyway. It's like being a ghost.

Yet Malchus got healed. It's been ratified. He has disappeared from the colony and my family told me why when they brought food. He went to a teacher called Jesus. If Jesus could heal Malchus, who was in a worse state than me, He can surely heal me. What's to lose in searching Him out and asking? My family told me that He is up the mountain by the lake. Maybe I can find Him out here in the countryside when He comes back down. Once He's entered a town or village, I'll have no chance.

> **8** When he came down from the mountain, great multitudes followed him. **²** Behold, a leper came to him and worshiped him, saying, "Lord, if you want to, you can make me clean."
>
> **³** Jesus stretched out his hand and touched him, saying, "I want to. Be made clean." Immediately his leprosy was cleansed. **⁴** Jesus said to him, "See that you tell nobody; but go, show yourself to the priest, and offer the gift that Moses commanded, as a testimony to them."

⁵ When he came into Capernaum, a centurion came to him, asking him for help, ⁶ saying, "Lord, my servant lies in the house paralyzed, grievously tormented."

⁷ Jesus said to him, "I will come and heal him."

⁸ The centurion answered, "Lord, I'm not worthy for you to come under my roof. Just say the word, and my servant will be healed. ⁹ For I am also a man under authority, having under myself soldiers. I tell this one, 'Go,' and he goes; and tell another, 'Come,' and he comes; and tell my servant, 'Do this,' and he does it."

¹⁰ When Jesus heard it, he marveled and said to those who followed, "Most certainly I tell you, I haven't found so great a faith, not even in Israel. ¹¹ I tell you that many will come from the east and the west, and will sit down with Abraham, Isaac, and Jacob in the Kingdom of Heaven, ¹² but the children of the Kingdom will be thrown out into the outer darkness. There will be weeping and gnashing of teeth." ¹³ Jesus said to the centurion, "Go your way. Let it be done for you as you have believed." His servant was healed in that hour.

OBSERVATIONS

I was the leper. I got healed. But then Jesus told me that I should go to the priest and offer the required gift, but tell no-one else. How could I do that? I had no money and was not allowed in the market. It seemed like an insurmountable problem and I did not know how to solve it. Maybe I should just have gone to the priest and they would have helped me.

24

DEMONIACS AND PIGS

CONTEXT

Following the healing of the leper and the centurion's servant, Jesus arrived at Peter's house in Capernaum to find that Peter's mother-in-law was sick with a fever. Jesus proceeded to heal her. Meanwhile word was getting around and the sick and suffering came thronging to Peter's door that evening, until the crowd was so big that Jesus decided that He and His disciples needed to leave the area. He told His disciples to get into a boat and having been waylaid a few times by would-be followers on His way to the lakeside, Jesus joined His disciples in the boat and they set off to the far side of the lake, presumably hoping for some peace and quiet and a chance to get some sleep. Jesus was so exhausted that He fell asleep in the boat, only to be woken by the terrified disciples, who thought they were going to drown in a storm. Jesus having quietened the storm, they arrived at the far shore, in the region of the Gadarenes.

MATTHEW 8:28-34

QUESTIONS FOR THOUGHT OR DISCUSSION

What do you think was wrong with these two men? Was it literally demon possession or would we want to call it something else?

What would have happened to the demons if Jesus had not given them leave to enter the pigs? (Luke 11:24-26)

What would the implications of the drowning of the pigs have been for the inhabitants of the nearby town?

Do you think Jesus owed the townsfolk an apology? Why would He not have thought so?

Why did the townsfolk ask Jesus to leave the area?

What does the townsfolk's rejection of Jesus say about their priorities and beliefs?

What did the events of that day say about Jesus' priorities?

Could it have ended differently? If so, how?

What do we learn about the Father heart of God?

COMMENTS

Everywhere Jesus went, His presence brought to light that which was not of His Kingdom. We will never know whether He crossed the lake knowing that He was there to heal two demon possessed men, or whether He really was hoping for a break from the pressure of all the crowds back home. Either way, He and the disciples arrived at the shore to find that a host of demons had seen Jesus coming and were exhibiting terror not of the storm, but of Jesus. The men were so possessed that it was the demons who spoke through them, rather than the men themselves. It is not uncommon for demons to manifest in the presence of Jesus, they know who He is and do not seem to be able to help demonstrating their fear. Their control over the men had been so dramatic that the locals had become too terrified to go near the area. Jesus was clearly completely unafraid, presumably because He knew that He would have the upper hand. One word: "Go!" was all it took. He gave the demons leave to go where they had asked to be sent and the pigs were drowned. That meant that an unknown number of the local townsfolk lost their livelihoods.

It is interesting to speculate on whether Jesus knew that the pigs would be drowned if He gave the demons leave to enter them. As God, yes, but as a human being possibly not. The alternative would have been to leave the demons wandering, but that would have meant them seeking a new home and someone else's life being ruined, or returning to their old home along with more demons and the men's sanity being lost all over again. At least this way the demons were presumably finished.

The townsfolk seem to have been less bothered about the men than the pigs. One wonders what track record the men had for violence, for which they had not been forgiven. Maybe the townsfolk could not imagine them ever being trustworthy again. Perhaps they did not really believe the enormity of what Jesus had done for them. Either way it is clear that they were very angry with Jesus about the pigs and did not want to know Him. Their priority was their own economic welfare, not the wellbeing of a couple of misfits. To welcome Jesus would have involved accepting the loss of the pigs and maybe even taking on board that He did not view pig farming as a legitimate occupation in the first place.

It is easy to imagine the townsfolk drawing the conclusion that the God of Israel did not love them, or at any rate, was not interested in their economic wellbeing. But there were conflicts of interest here and it is very clear from the fearlessness of Jesus' intervention that He had no doubt about His priorities, which reflected Father God's. The men's lives were being ruined by the demons to an extent that would never be true as a result of lost wealth, even if the wealth was not going to be replaceable. There is always a bigger picture than our own, individual vested interests.

MEDITATION

Jesus is exhausted. The disciples are reeling, they have never known a storm on the Sea of Galilee calm down so quickly, nor met anyone able to command such a thing to happen before. They are beginning to wonder who Jesus is. The demons in the men on the shore have no doubts about who Jesus is, they are instantly able to recognize Him. They have been having a field day since securing residence inside the two men. They have instigated violence and destruction, ensured total disintegration of the men's personalities and rendered them unable to hold down a job. Better still, they have had them banished from human society, glorious isolation the ultimate victory. No way are they relinquishing their victims. Let battle commence.

> [28] When he came to the other side, into the country of the Gergesenes, two people possessed by demons met him there, coming out of the tombs, exceedingly fierce, so that nobody could pass that way. [29] Behold, they cried out, saying, "What do we have to do with you, Jesus, Son of God? Have you come here to torment us before the time?" [30] Now there was a herd of many pigs feeding far away from them. [31] The demons begged him, saying, "If you cast us out, permit us to go away into the herd of pigs."

³² He said to them, "Go!"

They came out, and went into the herd of pigs; and behold, the whole herd of pigs rushed down the cliff into the sea and died in the water. ³³ Those who fed them fled and went away into the city and told everything, including what happened to those who were possessed with demons. ³⁴ Behold, all the city came out to meet Jesus. When they saw him, they begged that he would depart from their borders.

OBSERVATIONS

Pass.

25

JAIRUS'S DAUGHTER RAISED FROM THE DEAD AND A WOMAN'S HAEMORRHAGE HEALED

CONTEXT

Having been asked to leave the region of the Gadarenes, Jesus returned home across the lake. He reached His home town and some men brought a paralysed friend to Him. Jesus pronounced that the man's sins were forgiven, to the consternation of some of the teachers of the law who were present. They were incensed, as nobody but God can forgive sins. In response to their thoughts that Jesus was blaspheming, Jesus proceeded to heal the man, who got up as commanded and walked out. Then Jesus moved on from there, called Matthew to follow Him and stopped to talk to some disciples of John the Baptist, who were asking

Him questions. While He was having that conversation a synagogue ruler came and knelt before Him. Synagogue rulers were laymen who were responsible for looking after the building and supervising worship.[1]

MATTHEW 9:18-26

QUESTIONS FOR THOUGHT OR DISCUSSION

What was Jesus becoming used to from the Pharisees and Sadducees?

How was this synagogue ruler different from most trained Jewish leaders?

What would the social implications have been for the woman suffering from the haemorrhage? See Leviticus 15:25-27.

What was it that healed the woman with the haemorrhage?

What did the presence of flute players and wailing women signify? See 2 Chronicles 35:24-25.

Where did Jesus get His power from? (Matthew 12:22-37)

What do we learn about Father God?

Should we expect to be able to do what Jesus could do? (John 14:12-14)

COMMENTS

It is interesting to speculate on whether the ruler described here had been present at the healing of the paralysed man and if so, how he had reacted. We will never know. Either way, he had presumably seen, or heard enough about Jesus' miracles to have developed a belief in Jesus' capacity to heal. Faced with the ultimate need for a miracle for his daughter, he approached Jesus not only with faith, which he expressed as certainty, but also with humility. Jesus did not hesitate to respond.

On the way to the ruler's house, Jesus felt a woman touch His garment and turned to her to announce that her faith had healed her. That was an interesting comment for Him to make when it was His power that had healed her. And yet, had she not reached out to Him, she would not have received anything from Him. There is a similarity here with the power of electricity, which is residing in the wires behind the walls of our houses. It is invisible and powerless unless switched on. Just the flick of a switch can transform a dark room into a brightly lit one and we know when we flick the switch the effect that it will have, or we would not bother to do it. If we do not bother, we remain in darkness.

Can you imagine walking into the dead girl's house and telling everyone that she was simply asleep? Then holding your nerve when you were ridiculed? Jesus was so sure of His ability and authority, even over death. But as a human being He had no more ability or authority than any of us. He was totally dependent on the power of Father God and utterly sure of Him. He threw the unbelieving crowd out of the house. Then He just took hold of the girl's hand and she was raised from the dead. The news got around! If Father God could do it through Jesus, why not through us?

MEDITATION

Life around Jesus continues at a fast pace. In a very short space of time, Jesus has been proclaiming sins forgiven, healing people with incurable conditions, calling unlikely people to follow Him, defending His behaviour in the face of criticism from the Pharisees and explaining His behaviour and that of His disciples to John the Baptist's disciples. At the same time other needy people are seeking Him out. The leader of the synagogue has just lost a beloved child. We do not know whether it was an accident or an illness, either way it seems likely that it happened suddenly, preventing her father from seeking help before the death. He might not have been open to Jesus before this, but he is certainly open now in the face of his need. The woman has been bleeding for twelve years. That has meant twelve years of segregation from society, banishment from corporate worship, managing soiled pads, feeling drained from anaemia and with no hope of a reprieve. No way should she have been pushing her way through the crowd. Nor is the synagogue leader behaving in line with his peers. Somehow in their hopelessness Jesus' presence draws out faith from them.

> [18] While he told these things to them, behold, a ruler came and worshiped him, saying, "My daughter has just died, but come and lay your hand on her, and she will live."
>
> [19] Jesus got up and followed him, as did his disciples. [20] Behold, a woman who had a discharge of blood for twelve years came behind him, and touched the fringe of his garment; [21] for she said within herself, "If I just touch his garment, I will be made well."
>
> [22] But Jesus, turning around and seeing her, said, "Daughter, cheer up! Your faith has made you well." And the woman was made well from that hour.
>
> [23] When Jesus came into the ruler's house and saw the flute players and the crowd in noisy disorder, [24] he said to them, "Make room, because the girl isn't dead, but sleeping."
>
> They were ridiculing him. [25] But when the crowd was sent out, he entered in, took her by the hand, and the girl arose. [26] The report of this went out into all that land.

OBSERVATIONS

The word from Jesus to the woman was effectual and confirmed her in her faith, such that she knew that she had the healing she had sought.

26

TWO BLIND MEN AND A DUMB MAN HEALED

CONTEXT

Forming a picture of how blind people were viewed in Israel at the time of Jesus is not straightforward. Leviticus 19:14 and Deuteronomy 27:18 give a distinct impression that blind people were considered worthy of respect and that anyone who took advantage of a blind person by leading them astray on the road would incur a curse from God in consequence. In other words, blind people were understood to have God's protection over them.

That is not the whole of the story, however. Descendants of Aaron, who were hereditary priests, were not permitted to perform the priestly duty of offering food sacrifices if they were blind (Leviticus 21:16-23). Nor were the people allowed to offer blind sacrifices, (or sacrifices with any other defect for that matter, Deuteronomy 15:21). Added to this, blindness was on the list of curses reserved for those who failed to obey Yahweh, (Deuteronomy 28:15, 28). That is why, in John 9:2, we read of the disciples asking Jesus who had sinned, the blind man or his parents, that someone should be born blind. Jesus disabused the disciples of their assumption that sin had to be the cause when He replied that neither had sinned.

Whether because of the rules regarding sacrifices, or as a result of David's reaction to the Jebusites' taunt (2 Samuel 5:6-8), by the time of Jesus blind people were ostracized by society and forbidden to enter the Temple. Somehow, they had come to be seen as not fit to worship Yahweh along with the rest of the community. The psychological and spiritual impact must have been devastating, over and above the effects of the disability itself.

MATTHEW 9: 27-34

QUESTIONS FOR THOUGHT OR DISCUSSION

What is your understanding of how blindness was viewed in Israeli society?

What did the title Son of David signify? (2 Samuel 7:11b-17)

Why was it important to Jesus that the blind men believed that He had the power to heal them?

Why did Jesus ask the blind men not to share their testimonies?

Do you believe that dumbness can be caused by a demon?

What was the significance of Jesus healing blind and dumb people? (Isaiah 29:18, 35:3-6 and 42:1-9)

Why did the Pharisees need to accuse Jesus of healing in the name of the demonic?

What do we learn about the Father heart of God?

COMMENTS

Jesus has just healed a paralysed man, a haemorrhaging woman and raised a young girl from the dead and now a couple of blind men have followed Him back to His house. Jesus wanted to know whether they believed that He could restore their sight and they were quite clear in their 'yes, no buts' answers. That was enough for Jesus to grant their request: "Because of your faith, it will happen." (NLT) Jesus asked them to keep it quiet, presumably in order not to fuel the growing public movement which was putting pressure on Him to become the kind of Messiah that they were expecting and to bypass the cross in the process. He was also needing to lie low from the Pharisees, with whom a dangerous game of cat and mouse was beginning to develop. The men who had been blind took no notice whatever of Jesus' command to them and told everyone they saw throughout the region. How could they keep quiet following such a momentous event?

Then there was a dumb and demonised man. Jesus asked him nothing, after all he would not have been able to reply. Jesus just cast out the demon and the man became able to speak. The crowds had never seen anything like it, but the Pharisees accused Jesus of using the power of demons to cast them out. As if that would have been likely to work! As Jesus Himself pointed out, according to Luke, a house divided against itself falls (Luke 11:17-20). Vested interests are dangerous in the pressure to lie that they create and the spiritual blindness they promulgate.

TWO BLIND MEN AND A DUMB MAN HEALED

MEDITATION

Jesus and those with Him have been on a bit of a roller coaster lately. People will not stop appearing, pleading to be healed, some of them dangerous to be near. The storm was freaky too. There must be a break soon, but no, now there are a couple of blind people following behind and shouting for mercy. Can Jesus do what they are asking? His fame is spreading and the pressure is mounting. At last, the privacy of a house, but no, the blind men are not letting up. Perhaps they are not even aware that they have entered a courtyard!

> [27] As Jesus passed by from there, two blind men followed him, calling out and saying, "Have mercy on us, son of David!" [28] When he had come into the house, the blind men came to him. Jesus said to them, "Do you believe that I am able to do this?"
>
> They told him, "Yes Lord."
>
> [29] Then he touched their eyes, saying, "According to your faith be it done to you." [30] Then their eyes were opened. Jesus strictly commanded them, saying, "See that no one knows about this." [31] But they went out and spread abroad his fame in all that land.
>
> [32] As they went out, behold, a mute man who was demon possessed was brought to him. [33] When the demon was cast out, the mute man spoke. The multitudes marveled, saying, "Nothing like this has ever been seen in Israel!"
>
> [34] But the Pharisees said, "By the prince of demons, he casts out demons."

OBSERVATIONS

While I understand that it would have been impossible for the blind men to hide the enormity of what Jesus had done for them from their families and close friends, I felt grief that they ignored Jesus' command not to make it known and instead did exactly the opposite and spread the word everywhere. After what He had done for them, it demonstrated a lack of concern to please Him and a lack of sensitivity to His needs. It was not the best way to demonstrate gratitude.

27

CANAANITE WOMAN'S DAUGHTER HEALED

CONTEXT

Jesus has been travelling around Galilee healing people, teaching in their synagogues and talking about the Kingdom of Heaven. After this He returned to Nazareth and was met with offence and unbelief. Then He heard that John the Baptist had been beheaded, so He withdrew to a lonely place apart. However, the crowds followed Him there and He healed those who were sick and then fed five thousand people in the wilderness. Having sent the disciples back across the lake in their boat and dismissed the crowds, He went up the mountain to pray. He then joined the disciples by walking across the lake and Peter tried it too but panicked and sank, except that Jesus rescued him. They landed at Gennesaret and again they were besieged by crowds as the local people brought all who were sick so that Jesus could heal them. Then the Pharisees arrived from Jerusalem to question Him and were offended at His answers. In what might have been desperation, Jesus withdrew to the region of Tyre and Sidon.

It was the equivalent of going abroad on holiday to get a break, because anywhere nearer and Jesus was liable to be swamped with people making demands upon Him. He needed some time apart to grieve for His cousin and to get a good rest. John the Baptist was one of the first people to recognize who Jesus was and now he was gone, unprotected by God from injustice. Jesus must have known that He was in line for a similar fate and this would have made the prospect seem very real. He needed time alone to process all this with the Father and had not been able to get it. Meanwhile the disciples had no idea what was coming and still did not understand who Jesus was. He needed time to talk to them. He also needed time to recoup from the exhaustion of the ministry of the last few months. And to get anywhere they had to walk there, so they did, heading north across the border.

MATTHEW 15:21-28

QUESTIONS FOR THOUGHT OR DISCUSSION

What do you imagine that Jesus might have been thinking and feeling when he responded with silence to the Canaanite woman's plea for mercy?

Why did Jesus refuse the Canaanite woman's request when He did respond?

Where do you think Jesus was coming from when He equated the woman with a dog?

What kind of impression of Father God's heart for answering prayer do Jesus' responses give?

What did faith involve for the Canaanite woman?

What did faith involve for the disciples?

What did faith involve for Jesus?

What might faith involve for us in such a situation?

COMMENTS

It is not surprising that Jesus' initial response was silence. That is a common tactic employed by contemporary celebrities when people with no claim on their attention encroach on their privacy. Not only that; Jesus was in the habit of doing only what the Father showed Him, and this was not a straightforward situation, as He had been sent exclusively to the House of Israel, in line with a host of prophecies. He may very well have been silently asking the Father what He wanted Him to do. He also had a capacity for knowing what was in people's hearts and may have been looking at the woman to know what was in hers. He was in a difficult and embarrassing situation, much as a celebrity whose privacy is being invaded might feel today and even more so given the patriarchal nature of Jesus' culture and the fact that He was being approached by a woman, not to mention a Gentile. You just did not do what she was doing. Jesus' disciples would have been aware of this and their intercession to Jesus for the woman was along the lines of: "Get her out of here." You may never have prayed like that, but the author has to confess that she has and is not too proud of it, seen in the light of this passage.

Jesus' answer initially was to assert the fact that He was sent to the Jews and not to the Canaanites. This might sound rejecting of the woman, but it needs to be remembered that at this point Jesus was involved in an itinerant ministry, for which He had given up earning His living as a carpenter. He and His disciples were living on possibly their savings or else gifts from supporters, very likely a mixture of both. The situation could have been analogous to that of someone who is working for a charity, supported by donations. The people giving the donations know who the intended beneficiaries are and the charity workers have a responsibility to make sure that they use the funds accordingly. If the funds are insufficient to meet the needs of the people intended to benefit, there is a moral issue involved in stepping beyond the stated boundary. In such a situation Jesus had every good reason to state His boundary to the woman, given the overwhelming need in Israel from which He was trying to take a break and the fact that His commission from the Father was exclusively to the House of Israel. In addition, Jesus' initial rebuff to the woman could well have been an acknowledgement to a benefactor or two, present among the group of disciples travelling with Him, that they had justifiable reason to be telling Him to send her away.

The woman, however, was not so easily put off. She came and knelt at Jesus' feet, calling Him Lord and pleading with Him to heal her daughter. It is easy to imagine that Jesus would have been thrilled that she did this, as it allowed Him to keep the dialogue open. She had already called Him Son of David, which was a Messianic title and that would not have escaped His notice.

Jesus made the surprising statement that it was not right to give the children's bread to the dogs. In our world of anti-racist consciousness this statement appears questionable to say the least. However, everyone present would have been well aware of how Jews and Canaanites viewed each other. It was, after all, nothing new. Ever since Joshua invaded the Promised Land with the belief that the indigenous people had no right to continue to live there because they did not worship Yahweh and Yahweh was offended with them over their idol worship, there had been contention between the racial groups. Nothing much has changed. Think of how the Jews and Palestinians view each other today. Jesus was highlighting the elephant in the room in a way that everyone present would have known simply reflected the situation as it was. He was effectively saying: "Why are you coming to an enemy and have you thought about the implications?" Jesus would also have been acutely aware that if He healed the woman's daughter and the woman went back to her previous lifestyle as an idol worshipper, her daughter would be laid open to worse in the future. Remember the story about the house being swept clean and needing to be possessed with the Holy Spirit, lest the evil spirit that had been evicted should go and find seven other spirits worse than itself and the last state become worse than the first? (Luke 11:24-26). Healing is first and foremost about a relationship with the Healer.

The woman's response was not only surprising; it was profound. Only the dogs that belonged in the household would be the ones getting to eat the children's crumbs, not any other dogs. In her answer she was locating herself in the Master's household. She was effectively saying: "My loyalty is with You, not with my national identity, cultural gods or family's expectations of me." Jesus had found a way of enabling her to state this without entrapping her into saying anything for which she would invite reprisals against herself. He had also enabled her to tell Him where she was at, so that He and she both knew that He knew. What a master class in evangelism! Given that her statement must have thrilled Him, Jesus could not resist meeting her at her point of need, just as He delights to do for any of His Father's children. But to have done that without pulling any heart loyalty from her would in the long run have left her comparatively little better off. It is our hearts and relationship with us that He longs for and it is only in Him that we can find new life. It is tempting to think that Jesus' response to the woman's faith was about the fact that she believed that He could heal her daughter, but in fact her faith went far deeper than that. She not only recognized who He was, she was prepared to pay the price of loyalty to Him. She was remarkable and it was not lost on Jesus.

What does faith take?

For the woman it took the willingness to buck the cultural norms of her people and to run the gauntlet of misunderstanding and possible ridicule or even accusations of betrayal and death as the price of acknowledging Jesus to be the Messiah. But for anyone facing such a situation as the price of faith, be encouraged that Jesus will never turn you away.

For the disciples the challenge was the need for them to expand their horizon and to expect the impossible for the most unlikely of people. In their day the barrier to such belief was most likely to be the strict boundary they had around themselves in their understanding of themselves as the chosen race of Israel, over and against everyone else as inferior outsiders and not chosen.

For Jesus, as a man, it was to know His authority to heal with the power of the Father and presence of the Holy Spirit, by whom He was anointed. He promised His disciples that they would do greater works than Him and that He would anoint them with power from on high. He still gives His gifts to whom He will, so if we are willing to ask, we can expect Him to respond. The author has seen dramatic healings happen when people of God who know their authority in Him have prayed. In addition, she has been on the receiving end of miraculous healing herself more than once.

For us the challenge could be at any one of these levels. Are we willing to buck the trend of those around us who have no faith in order to remain loyal to Jesus regardless of what anyone thinks?

Are we willing to move out of our comfort zone and overcome our ignorance and fear in order to welcome those with whom we have nothing in common into God's family and by extension our own family?

Are we willing to step out in faith that Jesus can and will heal us or those for whom we pray and are we willing to ask for an anointing of healing in order to pray for others?

In the West, blockages are possible as a result of our scientific mindset and a loss of belief in the power of the spoken word. If we can recover the awareness that the Jews had that words have power and effect what is spoken, it becomes much easier to believe that when we say 'Be healed' under the authority of God and therefore with His power, He will heal, just as He effected the creation of the world with words.

MEDITATION
Imagine being on holiday near a beach and finding a favourite café with a fabulous view of the sea. You are chilling out having a coffee with your friends, when you are rudely interrupted by a complete stranger, from another part of the world, wearing national dress, with a screaming child in her arms that she cannot control. Not only does she completely disrupt the peace and quiet you were enjoying, but she has the temerity to park herself at the table next to yours and to proceed to butt in on your conversation. And choose what you do in terms of ignoring her and putting out sharp hints, she absolutely refuses to go away. Holiday over, even here!

> [21] Jesus went out from there and withdrew into the region of Tyre and Sidon. [22] Behold, a Canaanite woman came out from those borders and cried, saying, "Have mercy on me, Lord, you son of David! My daughter is severely possessed by a demon!"
>
> [23] But he answered her not a word.
>
> His disciples came and begged him, saying, "Send her away; for she cries after us."
>
> [24] But he answered, "I wasn't sent to anyone but the lost sheep of the house of Israel."
>
> [25] But she came and worshiped him, saying, "Lord, help me."

²⁶ But he answered, "It is not appropriate to take the children's bread and throw it to the dogs."

²⁷ But she said, "Yes, Lord, but even the dogs eat the crumbs which fall from their masters' table."

²⁸ Then Jesus answered her, "Woman, great is your faith! Be it done to you even as you desire." And her daughter was healed from that hour.

OBSERVATIONS

I found myself sympathizing with the disciples in their desire for peace and quiet and once the woman had gone, I found myself thinking: "Thank goodness for that, now we can have the break we came here for." In between, I felt that I failed to see the woman as a person and had little interest in her or compassion for her. She was just a stranger making a nuisance of herself and I could not see what good that was going to result in. Not a very comfortable experience!

Once the woman had located herself in the Master's household, what reason was there left for Jesus not to heal her daughter? She had effectively declared herself a would-be Israelite.

Had Jesus subscribed to the Gentile equals dog perspective, it is unlikely that He would have shown the woman such compassion and respect. He clearly thought differently from all those around Him and was unafraid to show it.

28

TWO BLIND MEN NEAR JERICHO

CONTEXT

Jericho was a remote village on the desert road between Jerusalem and the Dead Sea. It is possible that Jesus did not go there very often, as it involved an eighteen mile walk from Jerusalem. On this occasion He had gone from Galilee to the Judean wilderness beyond the Jordan and was on His way up to Jerusalem, a long, uphill climb, with Jericho en-route. Jesus' reputation as a healer and miracle worker was by now well established throughout the area and here was possibly a once in a lifetime chance for two local blind men. Whether they just happened to be sitting by the wayside begging or had come out specially as word had got round that Jesus was coming up the road we are not told. Very likely they were there all day every day, begging in order to survive.

MATTHEW 20:29-34

QUESTIONS FOR THOUGHT OR DISCUSSION

What were the blind men communicating to Jesus in calling Him Lord and Son of David? (2 Samuel 7:11-17, especially v16)

Why did the crowd try to silence the blind men?

What reasons might Jesus have had for not stopping?

Why did Jesus stop?

What did Jesus say and do?

What did the blind men say and do?

What do we learn about faith from looking at the blind men?

What do we learn about the Father heart of God from looking at Jesus?

What prophecy was Jesus fulfilling? (See Isaiah 42:1-9 and Isaiah 61:1-2, quoted in Luke 4:16-21)

COMMENTS

The two blind men were determined to get Jesus' attention and they were shouting out, calling Him Lord and Son of David. Both were Messianic terms, indicating that they were quite clear about who they considered Jesus to be. They were not going to be put off by the crowd and continued shouting at the tops of their voices and even more loudly to make themselves heard, regardless of the attempts of those around them to shut them up. It rather suggests that they had no doubt that they were in with a chance of a life changing encounter.

One has to wonder why the crowds were so intent on silencing the blind men. What were the crowds following Jesus for? If it was for His ability to restore people's lives, why not these blind men? Maybe it was less about Jesus and what He could do and more about themselves, wanting to be in on the action, whatever the action was. That might have meant trying to get near the front in order not to miss whatever was going to happen next. Anyone adding to the noise and making it even more difficult to hear would have been seen as a nuisance. It is as though they did not even see the blind men as people. The blind men would have been seen as social outcasts, much as lepers and demoniacs were, none of whom were able to make a useful contribution to society and all of whom were excluded from the Temple. Maybe it had not occurred to any of the crowd that Jesus could or would do anything for someone for whom they had nothing but ostracism. In addition, they had never seen blind people healed prior to Jesus' day. All of this makes it even more remarkable that the blind men had no doubts. Maybe they knew the blind people whom Jesus had already healed better than most.

Jesus meanwhile was on a long journey in a hot and dusty climate with more attention than He would probably have liked. He still had about eighteen miles to go before He reached Jerusalem. Most people do not invite hold-ups in such a situation. Jesus was different. He was also focussed on the needs of those around Him over and above His own needs. He stopped. The blind men could not see Him and maybe He could not see them either, although He would have been very tuned in to their need. He shouted to them above the crowd, asking what they wanted. All they wanted was to have their eyes opened! Such a request was no problem for Jesus. He must have gone over to them, or they were brought to Him, because the next thing we read is that Jesus was filled with tenderness—what a contrast with the crowd—and touched their eyes. Immediately the blind men could see and followed Jesus up the road.

MEDITATION

Have you ever been in a large crowd? Can you remember what your focus was? How did you view the people around you? As competitors for the best view? As nuisances if they made a noise and you had difficulty hearing what was going on at the front? As antagonists if they disagreed with you? As people to be feared in the event of a crush? As objects in your way even? Or as people with an equal right to your own to a good view? As people who might have needs greater than your own? As someone to facilitate or give way to? Your answers to these questions likely affect how you view the characters in this crowd scene near Jericho.

> [29] As they went out from Jericho, a great multitude followed him. [30] Behold, two blind men sitting by the road, when they heard that Jesus was passing by, cried out, "Lord, have mercy on us, you son of David!" [31] The multitude rebuked them, telling them that they should be quiet, but they cried out even more, "Lord, have mercy on us, you son of David!"
>
> [32] Jesus stood still and called them, and asked, "What do you want me to do for you?"
>
> [33] They told him, "Lord, that our eyes may be opened."
>
> [34] Jesus, being moved with compassion, touched their eyes; and immediately their eyes received their sight, and they followed him.

OBSERVATIONS

I pretended to be a blind beggar sitting by the roadside. I was determined that nobody should stop me from connecting with Jesus. Once healed, I did not want to lose contact with Him, so I set off to follow Him. Everything was very strange, as I had never seen any of it before. I also began to wonder what I was going to do when we reached Jerusalem, as I had no money and did not know whether Jesus would have time to pay me any more attention. It was beginning to dawn on me that there was a whole new life ahead of me, which would involve taking responsibility for myself in a way I had never been able to do in the past and therefore had no skills for. Although being able to see was amazing, I also felt quite challenged by the new possibilities in my life and fearful of the future.

Jesus was so alive to the needs of the people around Him, He never walked by without noticing. He reflected the intimate knowledge that Father God has of each one of us on a moment-by-moment basis.

Not only was Jesus aware of the people around Him, He also cared passionately about their suffering and felt for them. Not only was His heart touched by their plight, He was able to intervene to reverse it.

29

THE RAISING OF LAZARUS

CONTEXT
Mary and Martha's brother Lazarus was at home in Bethany and very sick. What to do? It is hard to imagine life without a health service, but they had nothing resembling the medical resources available in many parts of the world today. Their choice was most likely between natural remedies, recourse to a physician or a witch doctor for a fee or, unusually, to Jesus. He had a track record by this time for healing many, many people and word had spread. Not only that, but we know from Luke's Gospel that Mary and Martha had entertained Jesus and His disciples in the past, so they knew each other. Maybe they were related.

Perhaps the fact that Jesus had been happy to allow Mary to take her place amongst the men to listen to His teaching gave them the temerity to approach Him now.

Everyone knew that Jesus was on the other side of the Jordan, where John the Baptist had baptized people, for many were going out to see Jesus there (John 10:40-41). He had retreated into the wilderness following an altercation with the Jewish leaders in the Temple about the fact that He had been standing in the Temple at the Festival of Dedication and proclaiming: "I am the good shepherd. I know my own, and I'm known by my own;" (John 10:14). It was a Messianic reference to Ezekiel 34, part of the liturgy at the festival. The Jewish leaders were incensed that Jesus had made Himself God and took up stones to stone Him and then tried to arrest Him, but Jesus escaped.

JOHN 11:17-44

QUESTIONS FOR THOUGHT OR DISCUSSION

What did Mary and Martha hope for from Jesus when they sent their message to Him that Lazarus was sick? (John 11:3)

Why did Jesus wait for two days before responding when he received Mary and Martha's message? (John 11:6 and see Session 3)

How long did Mary and Martha wait for Jesus to arrive?

How did Mary and Martha feel about the timing of Jesus' arrival?

Did Jesus expect Mary and Martha to believe that He could raise Lazarus from the dead before He did so?

What did Jesus require of Mary and Martha before He raised Lazarus from the dead?

What was Jesus aiming to achieve in the raising of Lazarus?

What does the raising of Lazarus tell us about the Father heart of God for answering prayer?

COMMENTS

We do not know whether Mary and Martha realized that they were asking Jesus to risk His life in order to come back so close to Jerusalem. We can be sure that they were desperate. There is no mention of parents in their household, just three siblings. As women, Mary and Martha would have been dependent on Lazarus for their livelihood. Without him, they were facing destitution. They had to do something, and this was all that they could think of. All other potential remedies had presumably already failed and both the sisters were sure in their own minds that Jesus could heal Lazarus if He were to respond and come. It would appear that neither of them doubted for a moment that He would come. But Jesus did not come. For the sisters the waiting must have seemed interminable. It would take two or three days for their messenger to reach Jesus and get a chance to attract His attention. Hopefully he had got there safely and found Jesus. Perhaps Jesus had been waylaid on His journey. He must come soon. Lazarus was hanging on for Him for dear life. But still Jesus did not come. And then it was all over. Lazarus died before Jesus could possibly have got there.

There was nothing for it but to face reality and bury their brother's body. And weep and grieve. Neither of the sisters knew what they would do now to survive. It didn't even bear thinking about. Life seemed over. Certainly, life as they had ever known it was over. Why had Jesus been so far away? It could all have been so different.

The timing of Lazarus' death makes it likely that Mary and Martha would have been aware that Jesus had had no chance of getting there in time, He was too far away. Lazarus must have died within two to four days of the sisters sending their message requesting help. From the sisters' perspective, once Lazarus was dead it did not really matter when

Jesus got there or how long it took. It is easy to hear recrimination in the comments of both sisters, that had Jesus been there Lazarus would not have died. Given that they knew where Jesus was, that is unlikely. They were each expressing their complete belief in Jesus and that He would have been able to heal their brother had He not been so far away when they needed Him most.

Jesus was less bothered about what had happened and more interested in drawing out their faith to a new level of expectation. His proclamation to Martha: "I am the resurrection and the life" was a Messianic claim, designed to take her faith to a whole new level. When later she refused permission to open the grave, Jesus simply needed to remind her of their conversation and her assent to His identity. She then acceded and the grave was opened. Not before Jesus had been greatly moved by Mary's display of uncontrollable grief and had wept with her in solidarity with her pain, however.

Jesus' prayer at the opening of the tomb indicates that His focus throughout was on the opportunity for His identity as God's Sent One (ie the Messiah) to be made manifest. It is as if He already knew that the Father's heart was for the raising of Lazarus from the dead and had indeed known that before He had set out for Bethany. The raising of Lazarus from the dead vindicated His statement to Martha earlier that He was the resurrection and the life, the One through whom humanity would receive emancipation from judgment and the second death, eternal separation from God. Here was a Messianic claim epitomized in real life for all to see. It did not go unnoticed.

MEDITATION

At last Jesus and His disciples are setting out for Bethany, a walk of forty miles, a journey likely to take two or three days.

Meanwhile, as relatives of the deceased, Mary and Martha have had time to visit the tomb and inspect the corpse, to ensure that Lazarus was not just in a deep coma. It was customary to check on the body following a death, as two cases of people being found alive in their tombs were known, both of whom subsequently lived to old age. In addition, there was a Jewish Bible commentary that suggested that the soul did not depart from hovering around the body until the appearance of the body started to change, about three days following death.[2]

It is now roughly a week since Mary and Martha sent the news of Lazarus' illness to Jesus and they have had adequate time to certify that Lazarus' death was real.

> [17] So when Jesus came, he found that he had been in the tomb four days already. [18] Now Bethany was near Jerusalem, about fifteen stadia away. [19] Many of the Jews had joined the women around Martha and Mary, to console them concerning their brother. [20] Then when Martha heard that Jesus was coming, she went and met him, but Mary stayed in the house. [21] Therefore Martha said to Jesus, "Lord, if you would have been here, my brother wouldn't have died. [22] Even now I know that whatever you ask of God, God will give you." [23] Jesus said to her, "Your brother will rise again."
>
> [24] Martha said to him, "I know that he will rise again in the resurrection at the last day."
>
> [25] Jesus said to her, "I am the resurrection and the life. He who believes in me will still live, even if he dies. [26] Whoever lives and believes in me will never die. Do you believe this?"
>
> [27] She said to him, "Yes, Lord. I have come to believe that you are the Christ, God's Son, he who comes into the world."
>
> [28] When she had said this, she went away and called Mary, her sister, secretly, saying, "The Teacher is here and is calling you."
>
> [29] When she heard this, she arose quickly and went to him. [30] Now Jesus had not yet come into the village, but was in the place where

Martha met him. ³¹ Then the Jews who were with her in the house and were consoling her, when they saw Mary, that she rose up quickly and went out, followed her, saying, "She is going to the tomb to weep there." ³² Therefore when Mary came to where Jesus was and saw him, she fell down at his feet, saying to him, "Lord, if you would have been here, my brother wouldn't have died."

³³ When Jesus therefore saw her weeping, and the Jews weeping who came with her, he groaned in the spirit, and was troubled, ³⁴ and said, "Where have you laid him?"

They told him, "Lord, come and see."

³⁵ Jesus wept.

³⁶ The Jews therefore said, "See how much affection he had for him!" ³⁷ Some of them said, "Couldn't this man, who opened the eyes of him who was blind, have also kept this man from dying?"

³⁸ Jesus therefore, again groaning in himself, came to the tomb. Now it was a cave, and a stone lay against it. ³⁹ Jesus said, "Take away the stone."

Martha, the sister of him who was dead, said to him, "Lord, by this time there is a stench, for he has been dead four days."

⁴⁰ Jesus said to her, "Didn't I tell you that if you believed, you would see God's glory?"

⁴¹ So they took away the stone from the place where the dead man was lying. Jesus lifted up his eyes, and said, "Father, I thank you that you listened to me. ⁴² I know that you always listen to me, but because of the multitude standing around I said this, that they may

believe that you sent me." ⁴³ When he had said this, he cried with a loud voice, "Lazarus, come out!"

⁴⁴ He who was dead came out, bound hand and foot with wrappings, and his face was wrapped around with a cloth.

Jesus said to them, "Free him, and let him go."

OBSERVATIONS

Somehow, I had never imagined Jesus weeping with me over my losses before.

PART 5

JESUS, RELIGIOUS LEADERS AND RELUCTANT FOLLOWERS

30

LEAVE HOME AND FAMILY

CONTEXT

After Jesus had finished teaching the Sermon on the Mount, He came down from the mountain with a large crowd following Him. He healed a leper who approached Him along the way and as He was entering Capernaum, a centurion's servant. Then Jesus entered Peter's house and found that Peter's mother-in-law was lying in bed sick with a fever, so He healed her too and also numerous others who appeared outside the house that evening. The crowds still did not abate, however, so Jesus gave orders to go across the lake. On the way to the shore two people grabbed the opportunity to get close enough to Jesus to ask their questions. One was a scribe and the other was described as another disciple, suggesting that the scribe might also have been a disciple.

MATTHEW 8:18-22

QUESTIONS FOR THOUGHT OR DISCUSSION

Why do you think Jesus decided to cross the lake?

What do you think Jesus meant when He said that He had nowhere to lay His head?

Why do you think Jesus moved to Capernaum when He returned north, after being baptized and tempted in the wilderness? (Matt 4:13)

What does Jesus' reply to the scribe tell us about Father God's requirements of the scribe/desires for him?

Would Jesus' reply to the scribe have been more of a challenge for him than for some other members of society?

What was the other disciple suggesting to Jesus that he would like to do before returning to follow Him?

What do you make of Jesus' reply to the other disciple?

What are the temptations we might face to put Jesus second in today's society?

What does all this imply about the Father heart of God?

COMMENTS

It is worth considering why Jesus said that the Son of Man had nowhere to lay His head. Maybe He was simply issuing a challenge not to be too earth-focussed. However, in the light of what happened to Jesus when He visited Nazareth, there could be more to it than first appears. It is clear from the Gospel accounts that Jesus' brothers were quite antagonistic towards Him (John 7:2-9) and that the same was true of the villagers who worshipped in the local synagogue in Nazareth (Luke 4:16, 28-30). One can speculate that when Jesus became an itinerant preacher it caused quite an upset within the family dynamic. Up until that point He would very likely have expected, or at least been expected by the rest of the family, to continue to run His father's carpenter's business, especially as He was the eldest child. It must have caused a certain amount of unexpected stress within the family when He began an itinerant rabbinic ministry and He may have found Himself being deemed to have forgone any rights He might have had to the family home if He was no longer doing what was expected of Him to maintain the family income. We read in Matthew 4:13 that at the very start of His ministry, immediately after His baptism and temptation in the wilderness, Jesus based Himself in Capernaum, not Nazareth, when in Galilee. It is likely that He would not have had the same rights to that property as He would have had to an inherited family property. As Joseph came from the line of David, with his ancestral seat in Bethlehem and Jesus had been a refugee in Nazareth to escape from Herod when he was a child, He might not have been in line to inherit the property where He grew up anyway. So maybe it was quite literally the truth that Jesus had no earthly security in terms of a place to call His own and anyone who chose to follow Him would be taking the risk that a similar fate might await them. At the very least they would have to be ready to travel around with Him and could not expect to be based in one place while doing that, or to find places to stay in the wilderness or Jerusalem. Either way Jesus was issuing a stark warning that following Him would not be possible while trying at the same time to cling to earthly security and comfort.

Jesus issued a similar challenge to a disciple who wanted leave to first go and bury his father. We do not know whether his father had already died or was still healthy. It could have been a request for a temporary delay to arrange a funeral but was more likely for an unknown number of years to come. Had his father already died, he would not have been in a crowd surrounding Jesus in the first place, he would have been with his family. Either way it was part of the tradition of the Torah that caring for relatives was an important obligation. We read in Genesis 50:5 of Joseph requesting leave from Pharaoh to honour his promise to his dying father Jacob that he would return to Israel to bury him when he died. Later we read in Leviticus 21:1-3 that the priests were not to defile themselves while on duty by touching a dead body, unless it was that of a close relative. In other words, burying close relatives trumped all other duties, even priestly ones. However, in Leviticus 21:10-12 we read that for the high priest this exemption from priestly duties did not apply. Once consecrated, he was not allowed to profane the sanctuary even to bury his parents. As High Priest of humanity, Jesus is asking for no more, or less, than He has already signed up to Himself. It is very likely that Jesus was in effect saying: 'It's now or never,' knowing that His ministry was to be short lived and would end in His death. After all, He was never going to be able to bury His own mother. Jesus was challenging the would-be disciple not to put off following Him until his parents had died, but to be willing to leave his family, just as Jesus Himself had done. He was basically saying that following Him (Jesus) was so important and urgent that it trumped absolutely everything else, family loyalties included.[1]

MEDITATION

Jesus is in the local area and there are people everywhere, thronging around Him trying to get His attention, wanting to ask Him their question or to be healed. The crowd is jostling, getting bigger, impossible to ignore. It is incessant and exhausting. Jesus is in need of a break. So are the disciples. They are heading towards the edge of the lake and in the direction of a boat on the shore.

[18] Now when Jesus saw great multitudes around him, he gave the order to depart to the other side.

[19] A scribe came and said to him, "Teacher, I will follow you wherever you go."

[20] Jesus said to him, "The foxes have holes and the birds of the sky have nests, but the Son of Man has nowhere to lay his head."

[21] Another of his disciples said to him, "Lord, allow me first to go and bury my father."

[22] But Jesus said to him, "Follow me, and leave the dead to bury their own dead."

OBSERVATIONS

Nothing that Jesus ever asked of anyone was more than the commitment He was already demonstrating towards humanity Himself. As High Priest, His commitment towards the Father took priority over all else. So, the challenges that He issued to the would-be disciples were that they be willing to join Him, cost included. I found forgoing the support of family and friends a scary prospect.

31

THE PHARISEES' RESPONSE TO JESUS FORGIVING A PARALYTIC

CONTEXT

Jesus' attempt to get away from the crowd in Capernaum by crossing the lake did not result in much respite. He did get some sleep in the boat, but not much as the disciples feared they were all going to drown in a storm and woke Jesus up. Jesus rebuked the storm and it ceased. When they reached the other side, who should be waiting on the shore to greet Jesus, but two men possessed by demons. Jesus commanded the demons to leave the men and they did. He and the disciples did not get to stay long, however, as the local townspeople asked Jesus to leave the area. Sailing back across the lake, they returned to Capernaum.

THE PHARISEES' RESPONSE TO JESUS FORGIVING A PARALYTIC

MATTHEW 9:1-8

QUESTIONS FOR THOUGHT OR DISCUSSION

What was the response of the teachers of religious law to Jesus forgiving the sins of the paralysed man?

Why did the teachers of religious law think what they did?

Did the thoughts of the teachers of religious law constitute prayer?

How did Jesus respond to what He knew that the teachers of religious law were thinking?

What was required of the teachers of religious law to escape Jesus' verdict?

What would it have cost the teachers of religious law to change their minds about Jesus?

What reason did Jesus give for healing the paralysed man?

What does Jesus' response to the teachers of religious law tell us about Father God's heart towards them?

COMMENTS

Jesus was now back in Capernaum. Within days the crowds began to gather around Him again, seeking Him out, hungry to know more of what He had to say. Jesus was teaching them, when suddenly He found that there was a paralysed man lying on a mat at His feet. Had Jesus been one of the teachers of religious law (who had no power to heal), He might have been tempted to ignore the man and to carry on teaching in an embarrassed atmosphere. However, Jesus never ignored sick people who came to Him for healing. Nor did He fail to notice the faith in the hearts of those who brought this particular man. Jesus knew that the man's friends had gone to great lengths to get this man close to Him, indicating that they thought the effort worthwhile on account of their belief in Jesus' power to heal. Faith like that never failed to elicit a response from Jesus. Instead of healing the paralysed man, Jesus forgave him his sins and announced the fact in front of the crowd. The teachers of religious law who were present among the crowd, steeped in the Torah as they were, would have been especially sensitive to the fact that unless Jesus was God, He was usurping God's prerogative to forgive sins. Given that they did not think He was God, the logical conclusion was to question His temerity in pronouncing forgiveness for anybody's sins in God's place. Their logical conclusion was that Jesus was blaspheming by acting God. How often do people accuse others of what they are guilty of themselves! In refusing to acknowledge Jesus' true identity, the teachers of religious law were themselves guilty of blasphemy. As they had not yet reached the point when they felt the need to attack Him openly, they simply thought and kept their thoughts to themselves. However, Jesus knew exactly what they were thinking and called them out on it with a question: "Why do you think evil in your hearts?" In so saying, Jesus was both proclaiming His right to forgive sins and naming unbelief in who He was as evil. Then to indicate that He did in fact have the authority to forgive sins, He healed the paralysed man, who obeyed Jesus' command to take up his bed and go home, got up and went home!

MEDITATION

Jesus is back in familiar territory. Word of His presence in the area has taken but a few days to spread and there is another crowd around Him already. He is teaching the crowd and those present are listening to Him avidly; never have they heard such interesting and authoritative stories. Jesus is different somehow and people in the area are intrigued to know what that means.

THE PHARISEES' RESPONSE TO JESUS FORGIVING A PARALYTIC

9 He entered into a boat and crossed over, and came into his own city. ² Behold, they brought to him a man who was paralyzed, lying on a bed. Jesus, seeing their faith, said to the paralytic, "Son, cheer up! Your sins are forgiven you."

³ Behold, some of the scribes said to themselves, "This man blasphemes."

⁴ Jesus, knowing their thoughts, said, "Why do you think evil in your hearts? ⁵ For which is easier, to say, 'Your sins are forgiven;' or to say, 'Get up, and walk?' ⁶ But that you may know that the Son of Man has authority on earth to forgive sins"—(then he said to the paralytic), "Get up, and take up your mat, and go to your house."

⁷ He arose and departed to his house. ⁸ But when the multitudes saw it, they marveled and glorified God, who had given such authority to men.

OBSERVATIONS

Lying at Jesus' feet in solidarity with the paralysed man, it was such a relief to hear Jesus say that my sins are forgiven and to feel the possibility of living a life less bound by fear in future.

32

JESUS, LORD OF THE SABBATH

CONTEXT
Since challenging the teachers of religious law who were present when Jesus healed the paralysed man, Jesus has called Matthew and found Himself on the receiving end of more disapproval from the religious leaders, this time for eating with tax collectors and 'sinners' in Matthew's house. In spite of the animosity of so many religious leaders towards Him, Jesus responded when asked and brought the daughter of a synagogue leader back to life after she had died. He sent the twelve out to heal the sick in His absence and He responded to John the Baptist's messengers with a reference to the fact that He was fulfilling the prophecies

about the Messiah by healing the sick and opening blind eyes. Then He bewailed the lack of response that He had suffered from the inhabitants of Capernaum and other local towns. It was not only the religious leaders who were causing Him grief. Having returned from their mission, the disciples were again spending time with Jesus.

MATTHEW 12:1-14

QUESTIONS FOR THOUGHT OR DISCUSSION

What could Jesus have said to the Pharisees to avoid antagonizing them?

What was the significance of Jesus' references to David and the priests?

What was Jesus implying about the Temple and about Himself?

How did Jesus justify healing the man with a withered hand on the Sabbath?

Why did the Pharisees see such a healing as reason to kill Jesus?

Have you ever thought the kind of comments that the Pharisees were making, or said them to God?

In what ways does Jesus reflect Father God's heart, towards the disciples, the sick man and the Pharisees?

COMMENTS

Time has moved on and the Pharisees have become more vocal in their antagonism towards Jesus. On seeing His disciples plucking and eating ears of corn while walking through a field on the Sabbath, the Pharisees complained to Jesus that His disciples were breaking the law. Jesus could just have replied that they were hungry and was it not permitted to eat on the Sabbath, but He chose to up the stakes and took the opportunity to proclaim His relationship with the Sabbath. In aligning Himself with David, He was declaring Himself to be an anointed king, not yet on His throne. More than that, He went on to say that the priests in the Temple were not guilty when they performed duties on the Sabbath, and neither were His disciples for plucking and eating ears of corn. He justified His claim by declaring Himself Lord of the Sabbath and more relevant than the Temple. He was not only challenging the Pharisees for their rigid adherence to rules that betrayed the purpose of the Sabbath, which was for humanity's benefit; He was also proclaiming His identity to them. The Pharisees had such vested interests in their own positions of power and authority that any challenge such as that from Jesus was a threat to them.

Not much later Jesus was in the synagogue with them for Sabbath worship. There was a man with a withered hand present, so the Pharisees took the opportunity to challenge Jesus further on His view of the Sabbath. Jesus was well aware of their antipathy towards Him; but was not about to back off and protect Himself at the expense of someone in need of healing. Instead, He challenged the Pharisees about their own exceptions to the law when it came to rescuing livestock on the Sabbath and pointed out that a person was of infinitely more value than an animal. On the strength of that, Jesus then proceeded to heal the man's hand. He was epitomizing the truth of the saying that He had quoted to the Pharisees over the grainfield incident, that God desires mercy, not sacrifice. Jesus knew that their hearts were not right with God and was quite outspoken in His determination to tell them the truth about not only God, but also themselves. In this He was reaching out to them to repent, even when He knew that they were unlikely to do so and more likely to remain antagonistic towards Him.

JESUS, LORD OF THE SABBATH

MEDITATION

The disciples have recently completed an exhilarating mission. They have travelled round the area, meeting people they did not know, staying with strangers that in some cases have become firm friends and above all discovering that Jesus had enabled them to do the impossible. They have healed the sick, raised the dead, cast out demons, cleansed lepers. They are on a high, while Jesus is struggling with grief that so few people are repenting of their sin and falling in love with Yahweh. It is good to have some time together to catch up. They are wandering through the fields chatting, most likely on their way to the synagogue.

> **12** At that time, Jesus went on the Sabbath day through the grain fields. His disciples were hungry and began to pluck heads of grain and to eat. **²** But the Pharisees, when they saw it, said to him, "Behold, your disciples do what is not lawful to do on the Sabbath."
>
> **³** But he said to them, "Haven't you read what David did when he was hungry, and those who were with him: **⁴** how he entered into God's house and ate the show bread, which it was not lawful for him to eat, nor for those who were with him, but only for the priests? 1Samuel 21:3-6 **⁵** Or have you not read in the law that on the Sabbath day the priests in the temple profane the Sabbath and are guiltless? **⁶** But I tell you that one greater than the temple is here. **⁷** But if you had known what this means, 'I desire mercy, and not sacrifice,' Hosea 6:6 you wouldn't have condemned the guiltless. **⁸** For the Son of Man is Lord of the Sabbath."
>
> **⁹** He departed from there and went into their synagogue. **¹⁰** And behold, there was a man with a withered hand. They asked him, "Is it lawful to heal on the Sabbath day?" so that they might accuse him.
>
> **¹¹** He said to them, "What man is there among you who has one sheep, and if this one falls into a pit on the Sabbath day, won't

he grab onto it and lift it out? ¹² Of how much more value then is a man than a sheep! Therefore it is lawful to do good on the Sabbath day." ¹³ Then he told the man, "Stretch out your hand." He stretched it out; and it was restored whole, just like the other. ¹⁴ But the Pharisees went out and conspired against him, how they might destroy him.

OBSERVATIONS
Pass.

33

CEREMONIAL AND REAL DEFILEMENT

CONTEXT

After Jesus healed the man with a shrivelled hand on the Sabbath, the Pharisees were so angry that they began plotting to kill Jesus. Jesus knew and left the area. He travelled around, followed by large crowds. He healed the sick and told them many stories, about a farmer sowing seed, about leaving the weeds in a field to grow with the crop, about a merchant discovering a priceless pearl hidden in a field. Wherever Jesus went, the Pharisees turned up, asking Him questions and picking arguments with Him.

About that time Herod had John the Baptist beheaded and as

soon as Jesus heard the news, He crossed the lake in a boat, in search of solitude. He arrived to find a large crowd waiting for Him. He had compassion on them and healed their sick and then fed five thousand of them in the wilderness. Then He sent the crowds home and the disciples back across the lake, so that He could climb the hills to be alone and pray. In the middle of the night, He walked across the lake and caught up with the disciples. It was enough to convince the disciples that He was the Son of God. They landed at Gennesaret, where Jesus proceeded to heal more people amongst the crowds that gathered. Then some Pharisees from Jerusalem arrived.

MATTHEW 15:1-20

QUESTIONS FOR THOUGHT OR DISCUSSION

Did the Pharisees' tradition of hand washing reflect the law as recorded in the Torah (first five books of the Bible)? (Exodus 30:17-21 and Leviticus 15:11)

How and why had the Pharisees altered the law?

Why were the Pharisees so determined to discredit Jesus?

What was (and is) involved in honouring father and mother?

How had the Pharisees altered the command to honour father and mother?

How did Jesus respond to the Pharisees?

How does giving offence accord with love?

What do you think Jesus was hoping for from the Pharisees?

What was Jesus' verdict on the Pharisees?

How did Jesus turn the Pharisees' teaching around?

COMMENTS
Yet again the Pharisees were having a go at Jesus, this time because His disciples had not been observing the tradition of the elders, that they should wash their hands before eating bread. In the law there were a number of circumstances listed that gave rise to the need for the people to wash all over, such as being in contact with a dead body. Only the priests were ever commanded to wash just hands and feet, in the 'Sea' in the Temple, immediately before ministering sacrifices to Yahweh (Exodus 30:17-21). In addition there was a command for anyone suffering from a discharge to wash their hands before touching another person (Leviticus 15:11). The Pharisees had developed a tradition of handwashing for the whole population, not just the priests and those who were ceremonially unclean, based on a belief that hands were likely to be permanently impure and that what they touched would become impure as well, hence the need to wash hands before eating. Jesus responded with a question of His own, asking why the Pharisees negated the law of God with their traditions. He backed His question up with an example of how they legitimized evading their God-ordained responsibility towards their parents. This referred to the practice of Korban, whereby the Pharisees had ordained that anyone could make a vow to donate money to the Temple that they otherwise would have used to support their parents and that if they did so, they were discharged from their responsibility towards their parents. Jesus viewed this as hypocrisy and He upbraided the Pharisees for honouring God with their lips, but not their hearts, and teaching human ordinances in place of God's law. This goes quite against our British ideas of politeness, but Jesus was about telling the truth, as He longed for the Pharisees to realize their

mistakes and to return to Yahweh with their hearts. If He offended them because they chose to reject the truth, that did not put Him off seeking to alert them to their situation.

Jesus was also aware that the crowds had been listening to such Pharisaic teaching in the synagogues Sabbath by Sabbath and might not understand that the traditions about hand washing were obscuring the real issue. He turned the tradition on its head by declaring that not what goes into someone's mouth defiles them, but what comes out of it. Yet again the disciples did not understand and had to ask Jesus what He meant. While they were about it, they also asked Jesus whether He was aware that He had offended the Pharisees. His response was that if the Pharisees were not planted by God they would be uprooted and that they were blind and heading for a ditch that they could not see. He was absolutely clear about the spiritual realities facing the Pharisees and about the eventual outcome that they would reap and in the light of it refused to be threatened by them. Given that they were the nation's leaders and rulers, it must have turned the disciples' world view upside down, hearing the things that Jesus had to say about those in power and about the status quo.

MEDITATION

Jesus is surrounded by so many different people. The sick and needy keep on and on coming. For many of them, their friends and relatives are with them too. The disciples are keeping close. The women who are supporting them are also there. So many different people, with so many different needs. And then a group of Pharisees arrives, all the way from Jerusalem. The people make way for them. Given their self-importance, it does not take long for them to gain centre stage.

> **15 Then Pharisees and scribes came to Jesus from Jerusalem, saying,**
> **² "Why do your disciples disobey the tradition of the elders? For they don't wash their hands when they eat bread."**

³ He answered them, "Why do you also disobey the commandment of God because of your tradition? ⁴ For God commanded, 'Honor your father and your mother,' Exodus 20:12; Deuteronomy 5:16 and, 'He who speaks evil of father or mother, let him be put to death.' Exodus 21:17; Leviticus 20:9 ⁵ But you say, 'Whoever may tell his father or his mother, "Whatever help you might otherwise have gotten from me is a gift devoted to God," ⁶ he shall not honor his father or mother.' You have made the commandment of God void because of your tradition. ⁷ You hypocrites! Well did Isaiah prophesy of you, saying,

> ⁸ 'These people draw near to me with their mouth,
> and honor me with their lips;
> but their heart is far from me.
> ⁹ And in vain do they worship me,
> teaching as doctrine rules made by men.'" Isaiah29:13

¹⁰ He summoned the multitude, and said to them, "Hear, and understand. ¹¹ That which enters into the mouth doesn't defile the man; but that which proceeds out of the mouth, this defiles the man."

¹² Then the disciples came, and said to him, "Do you know that the Pharisees were offended when they heard this saying?"

¹³ But he answered, "Every plant which my heavenly Father didn't plant will be uprooted. ¹⁴ Leave them alone. They are blind guides of the blind. If the blind guide the blind, both will fall into a pit."

¹⁵ Peter answered him, "Explain the parable to us."

¹⁶ So Jesus said, "Do you also still not understand? ¹⁷ Don't you understand that whatever goes into the mouth passes into the belly and then out of the body? ¹⁸ But the things which proceed out of the

mouth come out of the heart, and they defile the man. ¹⁹ For out of the heart come evil thoughts, murders, adulteries, sexual sins, thefts, false testimony and blasphemies. ²⁰ These are the things which defile the man; but to eat with unwashed hands doesn't defile the man."

OBSERVATIONS
Pass.

34

DEMAND FOR A SIGN

CONTEXT
Following the difficult exchange that Jesus had with the scribes and Pharisees from Jerusalem about hand washing (or not) and honouring parents (or not), He and His disciples retreated to the region of Tyre and Sidon. It was there that Jesus healed the Canaanite woman's daughter. On returning to Galilee, He climbed a mountain and sat down and the crowds heard about it and started to appear, including numbers of lame, maimed, blind and dumb people, whom Jesus healed. After three days together in the wilderness, Jesus then fed four thousand people with seven loaves, before dismissing the people and sending them home.

Having crossed the lake to Magadan, He was again approached by the Pharisees and Sadducees.

MATTHEW 16:1-12

QUESTIONS FOR THOUGHT OR DISCUSSION

What did the Pharisees and Sadducees have in mind when they asked Jesus for a sign out of heaven?

What did such a question indicate about the Pharisees' and Sadducees' attitudes to Jesus' healing miracles and the feeding of the four thousand?

Would they have believed any other sign? (Luke 16:31)

What was preventing the Pharisees from believing that Jesus was who He said He was?

What kind of Messiah were the Pharisees and Sadducees looking for?

Why did Jesus call them evil and adulterous?

What was the significance of Jonah?

How did the conversation end?

What does this tell us about the Father heart of God for answering prayer?

Why was Jesus cryptic in the way that He warned the disciples about the Pharisees and Sadducees?

DEMAND FOR A SIGN

Why were the disciples slow on the uptake?

What did Jesus rebuke the disciples for?

What was Jesus driving at when He talked about leaven?

COMMENTS
The Pharisees were back, this time accompanied by the Sadducees, with whom they did not see eye to eye. The Pharisees taught a massive volume of oral, human tradition, embellishing the Torah (first five books of the Bible) and Prophets, while the Sadducees rejected all but the Torah itself and did not believe in the resurrection, which the Pharisees did believe in. For them to approach Jesus together was not something that He might have expected. It indicated that in spite of their well-known and entrenched differences, something in common was over-riding those differences. The something in common was a desire to undermine Jesus in the eyes of the crowds and to discredit His claim to be the Messiah. They were intent on tempting Jesus to prove His identity to them by showing them a sign from God, because they did not want to believe that He was who He said He was. Jesus responded to them with initial graciousness, acknowledging that they were well able to read the face of the heavens in order to predict the weather. However, He then went on to ask how it was that they were so unable to read the signs of the times, referring to the significance of His presence amongst them and to declare that they were an evil and adulterous generation, for failing to believe who He was. They would indeed be receiving a sign from God in due course, when God would raise Him from the dead, foreshadowed by what had happened to Jonah. Anyone who wanted to know and even those who did not want to know would remember what Jesus had said when the resurrection story broke, as Jonah was a familiar figure to all of them. Then Jesus departed from them. He was well aware of their antagonism and gave them all the space they really wanted.

Once alone in a boat with the disciples, Jesus warned them to beware of the leaven of the Pharisees. The disciples did not understand Jesus' view of the Pharisees and thought that He was talking about bread. It seems that Jesus felt the need to be careful, or at least memorable in how He communicated what He wanted to say to them. Maybe He was mindful that Judas was in the boat with them and did not want to hand him ammunition. Meanwhile the disciples were preoccupied with their lack of food and heard Jesus through the lens of their preoccupation. It took a while and a rebuke from Jesus for the disciples to register that He was talking about the Pharisees' and Sadducees' teaching. Given that they had nothing in common when it came to their teaching and Jesus was referring to them as though they did, the conclusion to be drawn is that the teaching in question was the discreditation of Jesus for not being a politically orientated Messiah, along the lines that everyone in Israel, including the disciples, was expecting. Leaven acts invisibly to permeate entire loaves and Jesus knew that the influence of the religious leaders would culminate in the crowds swinging round in support of them eventually. Yet again the antipathy towards Jesus on the part of the religious leaders of the day must have been a source of wonderment for the disciples.

MEDITATION

Jesus and His disciples have been on another long walk, northwards from Galilee to the region of Tyre and Sidon and back. Then literally thousands of people have flocked up a mountain near the Sea of Galilee to hear Him teaching and in search of healing, crowds that the religious leaders could only dream of drawing after themselves. And again, Jesus has fed them miraculously before sending them home, as His compassion for them meant that He could not bear to think of them fainting from hunger along the way. He has now come down from the mountain.

> 16 The Pharisees and Sadducees came, and testing him, asked him to show them a sign from heaven. ² But he answered them, "When it is evening, you say, 'It will be fair weather, for the sky is red.' ³ In

the morning, 'It will be foul weather today, for the sky is red and threatening.' Hypocrites! You know how to discern the appearance of the sky, but you can't discern the signs of the times! ⁴ An evil and adulterous generation seeks after a sign, and there will be no sign given to it, except the sign of the prophet Jonah."

He left them and departed. ⁵ The disciples came to the other side and had forgotten to take bread. ⁶ Jesus said to them, "Take heed and beware of the yeast of the Pharisees and Sadducees."

⁷ They reasoned among themselves, saying, "We brought no bread."

⁸ Jesus, perceiving it, said, "Why do you reason among yourselves, you of little faith, because you have brought no bread? ⁹ Don't you yet perceive or remember the five loaves for the five thousand, and how many baskets you took up, ¹⁰ or the seven loaves for the four thousand, and how many baskets you took up? ¹¹ How is it that you don't perceive that I didn't speak to you concerning bread? But beware of the yeast of the Pharisees and Sadducees."

¹² Then they understood that he didn't tell them to beware of the yeast of bread, but of the teaching of the Pharisees and Sadducees.

OBSERVATIONS

I found myself identifying with the disciples and feeling Jesus' rebuke, on account of my habit of making sure that there is a supply of spare tins of food in the flat, for example leading up to Brexit and also on account of recent preoccupation with colours and carpet for decorating the communal hall and stairs outside my flat door. Both behaviours betrayed a lack of trust in God's provision on my part and a corresponding lack of focus on the thing that is really important, namely loving God with all our heart, soul, mind and strength.

35

DIVORCE

CONTEXT

A great deal has taken place since the Pharisees and Sadducees last approached Jesus. Peter has declared his belief that Jesus was the Messiah and Jesus has started to prepare His disciples for His untimely death at the hands of the chief priests and other leaders in Jerusalem. He has been transfigured before Peter, James and John, performed yet more healings and taught the disciples many things about valuing despised people and about the importance of forgiveness. All of that took place in Galilee or north of it. Then Jesus left Galilee and went into the region of Judea, crossing from east of the Jordan. He was not far from Jerusalem, being followed by large crowds and healing many. His presence in the area was not lost on the Pharisees.

MATTHEW 19:3-12

QUESTIONS FOR THOUGHT OR DISCUSSION

What law did the Jews of Jesus' day have regarding marriage and divorce? (Deuteronomy 24:1-4)

What were the grounds on which Moses had allowed divorce?

Why did the Pharisees pick the topic of divorce to try to get Jesus to incriminate Himself?

Why had John the Baptist ended up in prison? (Matthew 14:3-5)

What was Jesus' initial response to the Pharisees' question? (Genesis 1:27 and 2:24)

How did Jesus interpret the law of Moses?

What does Jesus' interpretation of the law of Moses tell us about His attitude to women?

What does Jesus' attitude to marriage and divorce tell us about the Father heart of God?

COMMENTS

More time had passed and the Pharisees remained intent on tempting Jesus to incriminate Himself. This time they came without the Sadducees, to ask whether there was any reason that a man was permitted to divorce his wife. Bearing in mind that John the Baptist had been put in prison for criticizing Herod's marital arrangements and had ended up beheaded, this question was potential political dynamite. Jesus did not flinch. He went right back to the beginning and quoted Genesis to illustrate God's original intention for human marriage. But the Pharisees were not satisfied and asked why Moses had commanded the need for a written note of divorce. Jesus again did not flinch. In Jesus' day, there were two schools of thought regarding divorce. The school of Shammai interpreted indecency to mean marital unfaithfulness, making it the only allowable cause for divorce. Hillel, who lived from about 60 BC until AD 20, emphasized the phrase in Deuteronomy 24:1-4 about a wife becoming displeasing to her husband and interpreted that to mean that a man could divorce his wife if she did anything that he did not like,[2] even if she burned his food while cooking it. Jesus took the side of Shammai[3] and also put the so-called 'commandment' of Moses, which He described as permission, down to the hardness of people's hearts, which had made it necessary. He then went on to say that a man who remarried following divorce committed adultery, unless his wife had been unfaithful. In such a case it is clear that divorce was permissible, but ambiguous as to whether remarriage was permissible.

Women were apparently unable to instigate divorce and the idea that marriage should provide women with a loving and secure context for themselves and their children is notoriously absent from Hillel's approach. From the perspective of Someone who loved and forgave at any cost, the failure of human beings, including married couples, to forgive likewise must have been glaring and Jesus made no bones about it.

MEDITATION

The lines are being drawn ever more starkly. Jesus is continuing to heal people and the disciples have begun to realize that He is the Messiah. No sooner has the truth dawned than Jesus begins warning them that He is going to be killed at the hands of the religious leaders. He is talking to His disciples a lot about forgiveness, in fact He is turning their lives upside down with talk about greatness being closely tied to service. In contrast, the Pharisees are becoming ever more antagonistic towards Jesus.

Life is pretty full on. It has been a long walk from Galilee for Jesus and His disciples and they are in the wilderness, about a day's walk from Jerusalem. Near enough for people to come flocking, ever hoping for a healing touch. Or hoping to succeed in incriminating Jesus.

> ³ Pharisees came to him, testing him and saying, "Is it lawful for a man to divorce his wife for any reason?"

> ⁴ He answered, "Haven't you read that he who made them from the beginning made them male and female, <u>Genesis 1:27</u> ⁵ and said, 'For this cause a man shall leave his father and mother, and shall be joined to his wife; and the two shall become one flesh?' <u>Genesis 2:24</u> ⁶ So that they are no more two, but one flesh. What therefore God has joined together, don't let man tear apart."

> ⁷ They asked him, "Why then did Moses command us to give her a certificate of divorce and divorce her?"

> ⁸ He said to them, "Moses, because of the hardness of your hearts, allowed you to divorce your wives, but from the beginning it has not been so. ⁹ I tell you that whoever divorces his wife, except for sexual immorality, and marries another, commits adultery; and he who marries her when she is divorced commits adultery."

> ¹⁰ His disciples said to him, "If this is the case of the man with his wife, it is not expedient to marry."

> ¹¹ But he said to them, "Not all men can receive this saying, but those to whom it is given. ¹² For there are eunuchs who were born that way from their mother's womb, and there are eunuchs who were

made eunuchs by men; and there are eunuchs who made themselves eunuchs for the Kingdom of Heaven's sake. He who is able to receive it, let him receive it."

OBSERVATIONS

Jesus was concerned to protect powerless women from insecurity at the hands of powerful men. His compassion contrasts with the hardness of heart that could interpret Moses' concession as a command. The ability of women to instigate divorce themselves in order to escape from abuse was non-existent in the societal structure of the time. Vulnerability to abuse clearly was not in Father God's plan.

36

A RICH YOUNG MAN

CONTEXT

As far as we know, Jesus was still in the area of Judea, west of the River Jordan. Following the Pharisees' dispute with Jesus regarding divorce and Jesus' subsequent conversation with the disciples about the same topic, we read that little children were brought to Jesus, only to be turned away by the disciples. It did not escape Jesus' notice however and He welcomed them and placed His hands on them before moving on. Jesus' blessing of the children provides an interesting backdrop to the conclusion of His next dialogue and subsequent discussion with the disciples.

MATTHEW 19:16-30

QUESTIONS FOR THOUGHT OR DISCUSSION

Do you think that the rich young man thought that he had to earn eternal life?

How did Jesus challenge the rich young man's assumptions?

Did Jesus disbelieve that the rich young man had kept the commandments?

Was keeping the commandments enough?

Why did Jesus tell the young man to sell everything and give the proceeds to the poor?

What is the difference between keeping the commandments and following Jesus?

Why do you think the rich young man was sad?

When Jesus referred to a camel going through the eye of a needle, what did He mean?

What was Jesus really saying in verse 26?

Do Jesus' words in verse 30 remind you of the children He had given time to not long before?

What does all this tell us about the Father heart of God?

COMMENTS

The rich young man would probably have been a well-known figure, given that few people in Jesus' day were rich. He had kept the commandments, but was unsure that that was enough. The religious leaders of the day all had different ideas on what set of rules needed to be kept in order to be acceptable to God and the rich young man was wondering which of the versions was the right one. Jesus subverted all of them by returning to the original Ten Commandments. The young man had sensed that this was not enough however, so Jesus put His finger on what the young man lacked. To be completely dedicated to God, he needed to be free from attachment to his possessions. This left the young man sad, as he was indeed attached to them. We do not know whether the young man was grieving on account of not being found good enough, or whether he was grieving for the possessions he would be giving up in order to follow Jesus. Either way, Jesus let him go. Only the young man could make the decision necessary to turn his life around in a godward direction. Jesus loved him enough to upset him, as ultimately only complete loyalty to Jesus is enough. He does not seem to have required the same level of financial commitment from everyone, but He did require that nobody clung to idols that were taking God's rightful place in their heart.

Yet again the disciples had cause to ask questions and were amazed to hear that Jesus considered it difficult for rich people to enter the Kingdom of God. The disciples would have assumed that important Israelites, first among God's chosen people, would be first and foremost in God's Kingdom. For them not to even be able to get in according to Jesus' view, would have astounded the disciples. Their understanding of what it took to be good enough was based on people's Jewish credentials. Jesus knew that that was never going to be enough for anyone. He also knew that He was going to make a way that would reinstate the possibility of entering God's Kingdom as His gift to them, to be received in humility. Any camel going through the miniature gate into Jerusalem called the 'Needle's Eye' would have needed to unload and crawl through on bended knees.

MEDITATION

You are out in the desert of Judea with Jesus and a large crowd of people. The terrain is rocky, with sparse vegetation and very little shade. The Pharisees have been holding centre stage, in their black flowing robes and headgear, self-important and imposing. Until they were ready to leave Jesus alone, nobody else has been able to get near Him. Keeping them out of Jesus' way would be unthinkable, they are leaders and important somebodies. In contrast, the next people to reach the front of the crowd are quite the opposite. Small, unimposing, unsophisticated and unimportant in your view. Children are insignificant and should be treated as such. The disciples do not dream of not trying to protect Jesus from such time wasters. Jesus does not share their view it seems and yet again the disciples are finding themselves being backfooted by Jesus. There is not much time to assimilate that shock, as another important person makes it to the front of the crowd.

> [16] Behold, one came to him and said, "Good teacher, what good thing shall I do, that I may have eternal life?"
>
> [17] He said to him, "Why do you call me good? No one is good but one, that is, God. But if you want to enter into life, keep the commandments."
>
> [18] He said to him, "Which ones?"
>
> Jesus said, "'You shall not murder.' 'You shall not commit adultery.' 'You shall not steal.' 'You shall not offer false testimony.' [19] 'Honor your father and your mother.' Exodus 20:12-16; Deuteronomy 5:16-20 And, 'You shall love your neighbour as yourself.'" Leviticus 19:18

[20] The young man said to him, "All these things I have observed from my youth. What do I still lack?"

[21] Jesus said to him, "If you want to be perfect, go, sell what you have, and give to the poor, and you will have treasure in heaven; and come, follow me." [22] But when the young man heard this, he went away sad, for he was one who had great possessions.

[23] Jesus said to his disciples, "Most certainly I say to you, a rich man will enter into the Kingdom of Heaven with difficulty. [24] Again I tell you, it is easier for a camel to go through a needle's eye than for a rich man to enter into God's Kingdom."

[25] When the disciples heard it, they were exceedingly astonished, saying, "Who then can be saved?"

[26] Looking at them, Jesus said, "With men this is impossible, but with God all things are possible."

[27] Then Peter answered, "Behold, we have left everything and followed you. What then will we have?"

[28] Jesus said to them, "Most certainly I tell you that you who have followed me, in the regeneration when the Son of Man will sit on the throne of his glory, you also will sit on twelve thrones, judging the twelve tribes of Israel. [29] Everyone who has left houses, or brothers, or sisters, or father, or mother, or wife, or children, or lands, for my name's sake, will receive one hundred times, and will inherit eternal life. [30] But many will be last who are first, and first who are last.

OBSERVATIONS

The Father is so generous in His blessing and provision for those who are prepared to depend on Him. However, we cannot rely on our own resources, we have to rely only on His and let go of everything else. Jesus turned the disciples' world completely upside down. In the same vein I find it hard to imagine the possibility of my late, non-verbal, disabled sister being more important than the late Queen Elizabeth ll of the UK!

37

PAYMENT OF TAXES

CONTEXT

Passover was approaching and things were coming to a head. After talking to the rich young ruler who had sought Him out in the Judean desert, Jesus left the desert and made the long climb from the Jordan Valley up to Jericho and then further up to Jerusalem. He used the journey as an opportunity for private time with the disciples, preparing them for His imminent death in Jerusalem and teaching them about the importance of living as servants of others. On leaving Jericho, Jesus healed two blind men and on arriving at Jerusalem He entered the city riding on a donkey and was welcomed by the crowds with a carpet of coats and branches and a chorus of shouts honouring Him. The following day Jesus turned over the tables of the money changers in the Temple and then proceeded to tell stories to the crowds, which the Pharisees recognized were at their expense. They became even more determined to trap Jesus into incriminating Himself, so that they could arrest Him.

MATTHEW 22:15-22

QUESTIONS FOR THOUGHT OR DISCUSSION

What could the Pharisees have done had Jesus said it was wrong to pay taxes to Caesar?

What could the Pharisees have done had Jesus simply said that it was right to pay taxes to Caesar?

Why was the question about taxes so loaded?

Why did the Pharisees bring the Herodians with them?

What did the fact that they were able to produce a coin say about the Pharisees and Herodians?

What was on the coin?

What could Jesus have communicated simply by looking at the coin?

How did Jesus subvert the Pharisees' evil intentions?

What do we learn about Jesus as a human being?

What does this tell us about the Father heart of God?

COMMENTS

More time passed and nothing had changed where the Pharisees were concerned. In fact, they were increasingly determined to lay a trap for Jesus that would enable them to pass a capital sentence against Him and silence Him. This time they enlisted the support of the Herodians, who would have hated Rome and all that it stood for. Between them they came up with a politically loaded question. They buttered Jesus up with their recognition that He feared nobody in His pursuit of truth. Then they asked for His view on paying tax to Caesar, the last thing Herod would have been happy about having to do. Was Jesus going to side with Herod? Then they could have reported Him to the Romans for would-be insurrection. Or with the Romans? In which case they could have reported Him to Herod for treachery. There was no right answer possible. Jesus knew exactly where they were coming from and let them know as much. Then He asked to be shown a taxable coin. The Pharisees could not have produced one had they not been in the habit of handling such currency.[4] It had Caesar's image and inscription on it. Jesus could let His distaste of Caesar's declaration of himself as god on the coin be known without any quotable words, a facial expression would do it.[5] Then he turned the question round to His questioners. Whose inscription was it? Obviously Caesar's. In other words, it belonged to Caesar. Jesus then pointed out that Caesar was entitled to what belonged to him, but He did not stop there. He added that what belonged to God should also be rendered to God. This raised the uncomfortable question as to whether or not His questioners were giving to God all that was due to Him.[6] Jesus changed an either/or question into a both/and answer and in doing so silenced His opponents by putting them on the spot. Yet again He was speaking truth to power and was not cowed. Yet again He was challenging His antagonists to turn to God with their whole hearts.

MEDITATION

Passover is approaching. The Temple is growing ever busier and more crowded daily. There is a buzz of anticipation in the air. The Temple authorities are actively looking for a way to trap Jesus into incriminating Himself, so that they can arrest Him. Jesus is well aware, but is still in the Temple daily, teaching the people and the religious leaders and responding to questions from them. One particular story was about a King who became furious when the guests that He had invited to His son's wedding refused to come. The Pharisees knew that Jesus was pointing at them.

> [15] Then the Pharisees went and took counsel how they might entrap him in his talk. [16] They sent their disciples to him, along with the Herodians, saying, "Teacher, we know that you are honest, and teach the way of God in truth, no matter whom you teach; for you aren't partial to anyone. [17] Tell us therefore, what do you think? Is it lawful to pay taxes to Caesar, or not?"
>
> [18] But Jesus perceived their wickedness, and said, "Why do you test me, you hypocrites? [19] Show me the tax money."
>
> They brought to him a denarius.
>
> [20] He asked them, "Whose is this image and inscription?"
>
> [21] They said to him, "Caesar's."
>
> Then he said to them, "Give therefore to Caesar the things that are Caesar's, and to God the things that are God's."
>
> [22] When they heard it, they marveled, and left him and went away.

OBSERVATIONS

Pretending to be a member of the crowd, I found myself wondering how Jesus was going to bring in His own Kingdom with the Romans in the way and how His acquiescence towards paying tax to Caesar could possibly help. It all seemed so hopeless and unpromising and confusing, it was like a black cloud.

38

DEBATE ON RESURRECTION

CONTEXT

Jesus was in the Temple in Jerusalem, teaching the people in the run-up to the Passover. Earlier in the day He had been approached by some Pharisees and Herodians, intent on trapping Him into incriminating Himself, so that they could arrest Him. He astonished all those listening with the wisdom of His reply and the Pharisees and Herodians left Him alone. Then it was the turn of the Sadducees to ask an awkward question.

DEBATE ON RESURRECTION

MATTHEW 22:23-33

QUESTIONS FOR THOUGHT OR DISCUSSION

How would the crowds have viewed the Sadducees?

What did the Sadducees believe about the resurrection?

What did the Sadducees gain by their refusal to believe in the resurrection?

What was the background to the Sadducees question? (Deuteronomy 25:5-6 and Genesis 38:8)

How were the Sadducees trying to discredit Jesus and His teaching?

What good would discrediting Jesus and His teaching have done?

What did Jesus teach about resurrection?

How did Jesus interpret Exodus 3:6?

Why did Jesus refer to that particular passage in Exodus?

What impact would Jesus' answer have had on those listening?

What do we learn about Jesus as a human being?

What does this teach us about the Father heart of God?

COMMENTS

The Pharisees were silenced for the moment and the Sadducees took their opportunity to raise their own burning issue. They quoted Moses' teaching that if a married man died without any children his brother should marry the widow and raise up children for his deceased brother. This arrangement was designed to ensure that property was handed down through the generations and that the family entitled to it was not allowed to die out. The Sadducees came up with an anecdotal story about seven brothers who each married the same woman one after the other because each of them died leaving her still without a child. The Sadducees wanted to know whose wife the woman would be in the resurrection. Jesus was quite blunt with them. He told them that they were in error for two reasons, that they did not know the Scriptures, nor the power of God. Firstly, He told them that in the resurrection there would be no marriage. That meant no pre-arranged life-time circumstances controlled by parents. Then He addressed their refusal to believe in the resurrection by quoting from a part of Scripture that the Sadducees recognized as authoritative, (ie the first five books of the Hebrew Bible), when God told Moses that He was the God of Abraham, Isaac and Jacob. Jesus was quite clear that God was God of the living, not of the dead. He of all people was in a position to know! The crowds were amazed, as the Sadducees were a powerful and well-educated group of people and Jesus was a carpenter and yet more than willing and able to take them on. Jesus would also have known that the Sadducees had a vested interest in their refusal to accept the resurrection. If there was no future, there was no hope and not much point in fighting to bring about change. Maintaining the status quo and their own positions of power therefore became much easier to justify. But they were unable to answer Jesus and their attempt to discredit Jesus ended in them being discredited themselves.

MEDITATION

You have travelled to Jerusalem to celebrate the Passover, as you are in the habit of doing each year. The trip provides you with a rare break from the daily routine of growing food and struggling to survive. You are in the Temple, making the most of the opportunity to listen to teachers of the law more learned than you are. You cannot believe your luck when you realize that Jesus is teaching and you hang around within earshot to listen to what He has to say.

> ²³ On that day Sadducees (those who say that there is no resurrection) came to him. They asked him, ²⁴ saying, "Teacher, Moses said, 'If a man dies, having no children, his brother shall marry his wife and raise up offspring for his brother.' ²⁵ Now there were with us seven brothers. The first married and died, and having no offspring left his wife to his brother. ²⁶ In the same way, the second also, and the third, to the seventh. ²⁷ After them all, the woman died. ²⁸ In the resurrection therefore, whose wife will she be of the seven? For they all had her."
>
> ²⁹ But Jesus answered them, "You are mistaken, not knowing the Scriptures, nor the power of God. ³⁰ For in the resurrection they neither marry nor are given in marriage, but are like God's angels in heaven. ³¹ But concerning the resurrection of the dead, haven't you read that which was spoken to you by God, saying, ³² 'I am the God of Abraham, and the God of Isaac, and the God of Jacob?' <u>Exodus 3:6</u> God is not the God of the dead, but of the living."
>
> ³³ When the multitudes heard it, they were astonished at his teaching.

OBSERVATIONS

I was a member of the crowd and found myself catching my breath with delighted horror when Jesus told the Sadducees to their faces that they were in error and did not know their Scriptures. Nobody ever spoke to the powerful elite like that! Jesus had such assurance about who He was and such authority in what He said. At last I knew who to believe about the resurrection, between the Pharisees and Sadducees. Jesus went up miles in my estimation, He was so rock solid and my respect for the Sadducees diminished pretty completely.

39

THE GREAT COMMANDMENT

CONTEXT

Jesus was in the Temple in Jerusalem, teaching the people in the run-up to the Passover. Earlier in the day He had been approached by some Pharisees and Herodians, intent on trapping Him into incriminating Himself on the subject of payment of taxes, so that they could arrest Him. He astonished all those listening with the wisdom of His reply and the Pharisees and Herodians left Him alone. Then He was approached by the Sadducees, asking an awkward question about the resurrection. Jesus told them to their faces that they were in error, for knowing neither the Scriptures nor the power of God, something nobody else would have

THE GREAT COMMANDMENT

dared to say to them, except for the Pharisees. The Sadducees went away discredited. Then the Pharisees made another attempt to discredit Jesus.

MATTHEW 22:34-46

QUESTIONS FOR THOUGHT OR DISCUSSION

Compare verse 34 with Psalm 2:2.

What were the Pharisees hoping to gain by asking Jesus their question?

What did Jesus name as the greatest commandment? Look up Deuteronomy 6:5.

Where did Jesus get His additional answer from? Look up Leviticus 19:18 and Leviticus 19:34.

What does it mean to love God?

What does it mean to love your neighbour?

What were Jesus' questions to the Pharisees driving at?

Was Jesus denying that He was the son of David? Look up Psalm 110:1.

Why didn't the Pharisees answer Jesus' second question?

How would the Pharisees have looked in the eyes of the crowd?

What do we learn about human nature from looking at the Pharisees?

What do we learn about Father God from looking at Jesus?

COMMENTS

Many Jewish teachers in Jesus' day would have been in the habit of raising the question about the most important commandment in the context of their own teaching, referring to the 613 commandments included in the law of Moses.[7] Many would have agreed with the answer that Jesus gave. The Pharisees might have been hoping that Jesus would give an answer that placed Himself outside the mainstream of Judaism and left Him looking suspect as a teacher. Jesus did not oblige them, as His answer placed Him firmly within the mainstream of Jewish thought and the Pharisees would have been in agreement with Him. Any hopes that they might have had about discrediting Jesus as a teacher had He given a different reply would have been dashed. It is one thing to proclaim the commandments to love God and neighbour and quite another thing to live them out. Jesus' reply would have been a challenge for Jesus' hearers; Jewish teachers, the disciples and the crowds alike. Whereas the Pharisees were insisting to the people that they should be keeping such commandments in their own strength, whilst failing to do as much themselves, Jesus well knew that this was impossible. It was only through His resurrection life and the power of the Holy Spirit that anyone would be enabled to live out the law. And that is what He was planning to make available. Meanwhile He took the opportunity to challenge the Pharisees in return. Who was He? David's son or David's Lord? Or both? A partisan revolutionary king or King of the whole world? Defeater of human enemies, or Defeater of humanity's real enemy, that is sin and death? And if God, as He was claiming by implication, why did they not love Him by acknowledging that He was who He said He was?

There was nothing that the Pharisees could say in answer to Jesus' challenge and they were finally silenced. In failing to discredit Jesus they ended up discrediting themselves, as they were not prepared to accept that Jesus was the Messiah and as such, more than a potential political leader and ordinary human being. That is what Jesus' second question was driving at. Neither the Pharisees nor the Sadducees dared to ask Jesus any further questions, given they were so unwilling to answer His.

THE GREAT COMMANDMENT

MEDITATION

You are in the Temple during the week leading up to Passover, making the most of the opportunity to listen to teachers of the law more learned than you are. The place is heaving with people and there is a buzz in the air. You cannot believe your luck when you realize that Jesus is teaching and you are hanging around within earshot to listen to what He has to say. You have already witnessed Jesus discrediting both the Pharisees and the Sadducees with the wisdom of His answers. You cannot help wondering what is going to happen next.

> 34 But the Pharisees, when they heard that he had silenced the Sadducees, gathered themselves together. 35 One of them, a lawyer, asked him a question, testing him. 36 "Teacher, which is the greatest commandment in the law?"
>
> 37 Jesus said to him, "'You shall love the Lord your God with all your heart, with all your soul, and with all your mind.' Deuteronomy 6:5 38 This is the first and great commandment. 39 A second likewise is this, 'You shall love your neighbour as yourself.' Leviticus 19:18 40 The whole law and the prophets depend on these two commandments."
>
> 41 Now while the Pharisees were gathered together, Jesus asked them a question, 42 saying, "What do you think of the Christ? Whose son is he?"
>
> They said to him, "Of David."
>
> 43 He said to them, "How then does David in the Spirit call him Lord, saying,
>
> 44 'The Lord said to my Lord, sit on my right hand, until I make your enemies a footstool for your feet'? Psalm 110:1
>
> 45 "If then David calls him Lord, how is he his son?"

⁴⁶ No one was able to answer him a word, neither did any man dare ask him any more questions from that day forward.

OBSERVATIONS

Pretending to be a member of the crowd in the Temple and hearing Jesus asking how come David called the Messiah his Lord when the Messiah was rightly considered to be David's son was mind blowing. Could Jesus really be not just the Messiah but God, sitting there amongst all these crowds in the Temple? If so, the implications were quite scary, as the religious leaders were refusing to acknowledge Him and not for nothing, given that Rome would be horrified. But the religious leaders' job was to teach us about God. Jesus certainly seemed to be doing a much better job of that than they were.

Jesus could easily have walked away after giving the Pharisees a satisfactory answer to their question. Why didn't He? Instead, He asked them a question in return, which was designed to confront them with their unbelief in Him. Unless they were prepared to acknowledge it, there was no hope of them changing their minds about Him and that was what He longed for them to do. It was yet another way of calling them to Himself.

Initially I thought that Jesus had discredited the Pharisees, just as they had set out to discredit Him. He did discredit the Sadducees, when He told them to their faces and in front of the crowd that they were in error, although even then He was speaking the truth in love. This time it was the Pharisees who discredited themselves, in their public refusal to acknowledge Jesus as Lord and God, when invited by Him to do so. Right up until the end, far from trying to get rid of them, Jesus was calling them into fellowship with Himself.

Bearing in mind that it is not God's will that anyone should perish and that Jesus had already wept over Jerusalem that He longed to gather her people under His wings, but they would not, it seems rather more in keeping with Jesus' desire for intimacy with the people He created to see His comments to the Pharisees as an invitation to relationship, rather than an attempt just to get rid of them.

PART 6

JESUS, THE CIVIC AUTHORITIES AND THE CROSS

THE LAST WEEK OF JESUS' LIFE

A range of people initiated interaction with Jesus shortly before His arrest and during His trial and crucifixion. They included the civic authorities, that is the Roman Governor Pilate and the Roman soldiers, a largely hated occupying force, who bar one needy centurion have not featured in conversation with Jesus in the Gospel records prior to this point. There were also Mary of Bethany, a couple of the disciples and Jesus' mother, the religious leaders and a needy criminal, together representative of each of the groups of people we have already encountered. Because of the intensely dramatic nature of the last week of Jesus' life, they have been grouped together around the events leading up to His death and resurrection.

Prayer is here in Part 6, as also in Part 5, being defined as interacting with God, whether positively or negatively. This could be viewed as stretching the point regarding the definition of prayer, which is traditionally viewed as positive interaction with God. However, our human hearts are not always as pure as we might like to imagine, so including people who found themselves out of their depth or antagonistic when face to face with Jesus allows for identification by those who might find themselves unwittingly in sympathy with the 'wrong' people. This can provide a wake-up call for the need to turn back to God.

40

MARY OF BETHANY ANOINTING JESUS WITH PERFUME

CONTEXT

It was winter and Jesus went to Jerusalem for the Festival of Dedication. One of the readings in the Temple liturgy for the festival would have been Ezekiel 34, a passage describing Yahweh's anger with the false shepherds of Israel and His promise to shepherd His people Israel Himself. So when Jesus announced in the Temple that He was the Good Shepherd, the Jews would have been aware that He was making a claim that He was God. They were divided in their opinion about Him and accosted Him in the Temple at the festival, demanding that He tell them plainly who He was. In their view His answer amounted to blasphemy and they tried to stone Him. Jesus therefore withdrew to the wilderness beyond the Jordon, only returning briefly to Bethany in order to respond to Mary and Martha's message that their brother Lazarus was sick. Many Jews from Jerusalem were there in Bethany, supporting Mary and Martha in their grief, so once having raised Lazarus from the dead, Jesus withdrew back into the wilderness.

Six days before the Passover Jesus arrived back in Bethany and was invited to dinner at the home of Simon the leper. It was not far from Mary and Martha's house. John tells us in his Gospel that Martha was present at the dinner, helping Simon out by serving at his table. The sisters had probably already agreed that their most valuable possession could be used to benefit and bless Jesus. This was an alabaster phial of very expensive perfume, which they possibly kept buried in their yard for safety's sake. It is unlikely that they would have been able to afford to buy such an expensive item, it was worth a year's wages. Maybe it had been given to them, but we do not know for sure, we are not told.

Matthew, writing earlier than John, omits the names of the people he was writing about. Very probably they were still alive and needed protecting from the authorities. John wrote much later, by which time it is likely that the people he named had all died. The passages augment each other, so it is worth looking at them together.

MATTHEW 26:6-13 AND JOHN 12:1-8

QUESTIONS FOR THOUGHT OR DISCUSSION

What was the history of Mary's relationship with Jesus? (Luke 10:38-42 and John 11:28-44)

Why did Mary think that Jesus might appreciate having perfume poured over Him?

MARY OF BETHANY ANOINTING JESUS WITH PERFUME

What did Mary's gift to Jesus cost her?

What obstacles stood in the way of Mary being able to reach Jesus with the perfume?

What risks did Mary have to take?

What objections were raised to Mary's action and by whom?

Why were the objections raised?

How might Jesus have felt about the objections?

What was Jesus' response to the objectors and to Mary?

What does Jesus' response tell us about Father God?

In what sense was Mary's action a prayer?

Is there any way in which we can emulate Mary now? (Romans 12:1)

COMMENTS

Mary probably knew Jesus quite well. Bethany was a convenient stopping place on the route up to Jerusalem and she and Martha were willing to offer hospitality. Mary found Jesus' teaching fascinating and could not resist listening in when she got the opportunity. It had wound Martha up, but Jesus had made no attempt to prevent Mary from joining the men and paying Him attention. In fact He had welcomed her. So when their brother Lazarus became ill, Mary and Martha had sent word to Jesus, hoping that He would come when they needed Him. They both had faith that Jesus was the Messiah and that He could heal their brother. In the event they received Lazarus back from the dead, beyond any expectation that either of them had about what Jesus could do. Had they lost Lazarus, they would have had nobody to depend on and the perfume that they owned would have had to be sold to enable them to survive. But that did not happen and they were not left destitute, thanks to Jesus. Their appreciation for Jesus knew no bounds, but how they could ever repay Him was beyond them. Until Mary remembered that Jesus had been repeatedly warning His disciples that He would not be with them for much longer. She had heard Him herself, while sitting at His feet and listening to Him while He was teaching. Maybe she could anoint Him ready for burial.

Mary saw her chance. Jesus was close by and reclining in a neighbour's house. The perfect opportunity. Hopefully the fact that He had not turned her away when she joined the men to listen to Him when He had visited them would mean that He would not turn her away now. Hopefully too, the fact that Jesus had been so in tune with her feelings after Lazarus had died and shown her such empathy and compassion would mean that He would understand the adoration and gratitude behind her gesture. She would have to intrude uninvited into Simon's party and run the gauntlet of the men, but the relationship that she had with Jesus made the risk worth it. Plus, she had a feeling that it would be now or never. If He was ever going to know how grateful she was for Lazarus, it was now, while He was still alive. And He would need the perfume if what she feared was coming turned out to be true. Nothing for it but to take the risk.

The reactions that Mary dreaded were not long in coming. "Why this waste? For this ointment might have been sold for much and given to the poor." She must have felt so belittled, misunderstood, devalued, hurt. Jesus had every reason to feel hurt too, that His disciples begrudged Him such costly devotion. However, He gave no indication of it. Rather, His focus was on what was happening to Mary, not on His own hurt. He returned the disciples' question with one of His own: "Why berate her for doing such a good thing to me?" (NLT) Jesus had affirmed what she had done, as she had so hoped that He would. Then confirmation of what she had suspected, still being denied by the disciples: "You will always have the poor among you, but I will not be here with you much longer. She has poured this perfume on me to prepare my body for burial. I assure you, wherever the Good News is preached throughout the world, this woman's deed will be talked about in her memory." (NLT) Jesus had accepted Mary's offering and taken the opportunity to further prepare His disciples for what was coming.

Jesus was so different. Mary so wanted to stay in His presence. But she could not stay, she was in Simon's house and there was no welcome for her there from him or any of the men. She had to leave and quickly. But Jesus had stuck up for her against everyone else in the room. He had understood and appreciated her gesture. She had suspected that He would not spurn her or reject her gift and she had been proved right. She had also been proved right in her suspicion that it had been now or never, that Jesus wasn't going to be with them for much longer. She did not understand it, she just knew that that was what He had been telling His disciples when He visited her house and she had joined the men to listen to what He was saying. It was strange that the disciples did not appear to believe Him. Or maybe they did not want to hear it, because it was so far removed from their own vision for the future. Anyway, if Jesus was going to die, her perfume could not have been better used. He was worth it. He had raised Lazarus from the dead, saved her from destitution and accorded her respect as a human being.

Jesus knew, as Mary did not quite yet, that it would make such a difference to the experience of being crucified. It would mask the stench of sweat and blood and excrement. And her appreciation of Him would counteract the hatred of the Jews and contempt of the Romans. And her action would make sense to the disciples once He had been crucified and raised from the dead and they would remember and record it. Mary did not know any of that yet. She could not possibly have imagined that her name would be being remembered two thousand years hence. What did Jesus mean that what she had done would be told in her memory? It was the least she could have done. But now she was going to be famous! Jesus had transformed her sense of worth completely, beyond anything she had imagined or ever hoped for. Life would never be the same again.

MEDITATION

Mary dug the phial out of the ground in the yard and washed the mud off. Then she tucked it into her clothing and set off up the village to Simon's house. She could hear the buzz of conversation coming through the windows and smell the food. Weren't the men privileged to be able to lounge around together over a meal like this! Normally her only chance of being in on the act was by joining Martha at the serving. Something she hated doing and was not very good at. But today was not a normal day. She had taken some time out because she was about to anoint Jesus with her most precious possession, the most expensive perfume she might ever own. She stopped outside the door and leaned against the wall to make herself invisible. Glancing in the direction of the window she was able to make out whereabouts in the room Jesus was reclining. She plucked up her courage and entered the house, creeping round behind the men until she reached Jesus. She had made it. She was standing behind Him. You are wondering what is going to happen next.

MATTHEW 26

⁶ Now when Jesus was in Bethany, in the house of Simon the leper, ⁷ a woman came to him having an alabaster jar of very expensive ointment, and she poured it on his head as he sat at the table. ⁸ But when his disciples saw this, they were indignant, saying, "Why this waste? ⁹ For this ointment might have been sold for much and given to the poor."

¹⁰ However, knowing this, Jesus said to them, "Why do you trouble the woman? She has done a good work for me. ¹¹ For you always have the poor with you, but you don't always have me. ¹² For in pouring this ointment on my body, she did it to prepare me for burial. ¹³ Most certainly I tell you, wherever this Good News is preached in the whole world, what this woman has done will also be spoken of as a memorial of her."

MARY OF BETHANY ANOINTING JESUS WITH PERFUME

JOHN 12

12 Then six days before the Passover, Jesus came to Bethany, where Lazarus was, who had been dead, whom he raised from the dead. ² So they made him a supper there. Martha served, but Lazarus was one of those who sat at the table with him. ³ Therefore Mary took a pound of ointment of pure nard, very precious, and anointed Jesus's feet and wiped his feet with her hair. The house was filled with the fragrance of the ointment. ⁴ Then Judas Iscariot, Simon's son, one of his disciples, who would betray him, said, ⁵ "Why wasn't this ointment sold for three hundred denarii, and given to the poor?" ⁶ Now he said this, not because he cared for the poor, but because he was a thief, and having the money box, used to steal what was put into it. ⁷ But Jesus said, "Leave her alone. She has kept this for the day of my burial. ⁸ For you always have the poor with you, but you don't always have me."

OBSERVATIONS

Jesus honoured Mary in response to the fact that she had honoured Him. That was in such contrast to the way that the men of Mary's generation treated her.

41

JUDAS

CONTEXT

Jesus had aroused the antagonism of the Pharisees and Sadducees by proclaiming Himself to be the Good Shepherd at a festival in Jerusalem, a Messianic claim not lost on the religious leaders and Temple authorities. He had raised Lazarus from the dead and attracted many followers among the inhabitants of Jerusalem as a result. This was made manifest when He entered Jerusalem riding on a donkey, to the acclaim of the crowds. He turned over the tables of the money changers and taught in the Temple, further arousing the antagonism of the religious leaders. The religious leaders were threatened by Jesus' popularity and apparent disregard for Rome's authority and furious that He told so many stories that they recognized to be at their expense. They were actively seeking a way to have Jesus arrested and killed and Jesus was well aware of the danger that He was in. The disciples were less aware, but must have sensed that it was becoming risky to be known as a follower of Jesus. Jesus refused to run away however and remained in Jerusalem to celebrate the Passover, retiring at night, after a Passover meal, to a favourite haunt on the Mount of Olives.

MATTHEW 26:47-56

QUESTIONS FOR THOUGHT OR DISCUSSION

What might Judas' motivation have been for betraying Jesus?

What made Judas similar to/different from the rest of the disciples?

What was the temptation that tested Judas?

How did Judas react to temptation?

What temptation had Jesus been facing? (Matthew 26:36-46)

How did Jesus respond to temptation?

How did at least one disciple react to Jesus' arrest?

What were the wrongs involved in Jesus' arrest and His disciples' reactions?

How did Jesus respond to the wrongs?

What was Jesus' understanding of the significance of His arrest?

What does this tell us about Jesus?

What does this tell us about the Father heart of God?

COMMENTS
One has to wonder what was going on for Judas. We read later on that when he realized that Jesus had been condemned to death following His arrest, Judas returned the money and killed himself. Did he imagine that something less bad would happen to Jesus, given that He was guilty of nothing deserving of death, or had Judas not even thought that far ahead? And what were his motives in the first place? We know that he held the common purse and that it was known, at least subsequently, that he was in the habit of helping himself to some of the money. This rather suggests that money had a hold on his heart and that Jesus did not have first place in his affections. The implications may well not have been apparent to him. The disciples did not understand Jesus' destiny in advance of the crucifixion, nor were they open to Jesus' numerous warnings of what was to come. They had struggled to take in who He was and very likely Judas had not processed that if Jesus was the Messiah, the command to love the Lord your God and not to commit idolatry applied to his relationship with Jesus every bit as much as to his relationship with Yahweh.

We know that the Jewish leaders were seeking a way to put Jesus to death and they may well have looked to His followers for help with this. Faced with an opportunity to make some money, Judas may have found it tempting, if his love for money was stronger than his love for Jesus. Maybe he was also becoming afraid of being known as a follower of Jesus in a political climate that was anything but favourable towards Him. The temptation to save his own life by distancing himself from Jesus in the eyes of the authorities might have felt even more pressing than the lure of money. Maybe Judas just did not understand what Jesus was about and thought that He had lost credibility. If he did not trust Him, why would he want to continue to be associated with Him, when it was clearly becoming so risky?

Jesus made no attempt to resist the attacks against Him. He gave every indication of knowing why Judas had come to Gethsemane and what his intention was. Even so He called him 'comrade/friend.' Judas' kiss for Jesus was an outward show of affection, but it was not matched by what was in Judas' heart. Jesus was well aware and He did not kiss Judas back, rather He gave him space to do what he wanted to do. Jesus' comment, which is difficult to translate from the Greek, could have meant 'For *this* you come!'—an expression of disappointment in Judas and resignation to the Father's will.[1] In contrast, Jesus put a stop to His follower's reaction when he cut off the ear of the high priest's slave, which was self-defensive and designed to risk a nasty fight. Jesus resisted the temptation to defend Himself, but was quick to protect a slave that one of His followers had designated in his mind as enemy. In so doing, Jesus rejected physical force as a means to usher in His kingdom. Long before this Jesus had settled in His mind that the fulfilment of His mission required Him to accept an unjust death sentence for speaking the truth. That was what the temptation in the wilderness was all about and Jesus won the battle. He had to fight the battle all over again in Gethsemane and again He won it. Now He was free to live out His victory, out of love and loyalty to His Father. He was also in control of the situation and aware that He was not in any danger that was not under the Father's control and from which He could not be rescued. He was utterly secure in the Father's love for Him. He could have asked for twelve legions of angels to rescue Him, but chose not to. That would have been a host of angels, at six thousand per legion. He preferred rather to suffer for the benefit of all the antagonists around Him, as well as the rest of the world. He took the opportunity to point out to the arrest party that coming against Him as though He were a criminal should hardly have been necessary, given His easy accessibility to them while He was teaching in the Temple. He was letting them know that He knew that they were afraid of the people and acting in a cowardly fashion, as they had no justifiable reason for arresting Him, but that what they were doing was in fulfilment of the Scriptures, a necessity if God's faithfulness was to be upheld. When the disciples realized what was happening, they were terrified for their own lives and deserted Jesus and fled.

MEDITATION

It has been a long evening, celebrating a Passover meal in an upstairs, secret venue. Jesus has shared a great deal of what was on His mind and it has been hard to take it all in. It is late and time to retire, which means a short walk around the outside of the walls of Jerusalem and up the Kidron Valley to the Mount of Olives and a private cave, which will offer some security for the night. Jesus is not ready to fall asleep however, He asks for support while He stays up and prays. The prayer is long and agonizing, but nobody else manages to stay awake for long enough to support Jesus through it. The third time that Jesus returned to the others, He told them to wake up and get up.

> [47] While he was still speaking, behold, Judas, one of the twelve, came, and with him a great multitude with swords and clubs, from the chief priests and elders of the people. [48] Now he who betrayed him had given them a sign, saying, "Whoever I kiss, he is the one. Seize him." [49] Immediately he came to Jesus, and said, "Greetings, Rabbi!" and kissed him.
>
> [50] Jesus said to him, "Friend, why are you here?"
>
> Then they came and laid hands on Jesus, and took him. [51] Behold, one of those who were with Jesus stretched out his hand and drew his sword, and struck the servant of the high priest, and cut off his ear.
>
> [52] Then Jesus said to him, "Put your sword back into its place, for all those who take the sword will die by the sword. [53] Or do you think

that I couldn't ask my Father, and he would even now send me more than twelve legions of angels? [54] How then would the Scriptures be fulfilled that it must be so?"

[55] In that hour Jesus said to the multitudes, "Have you come out as against a robber with swords and clubs to seize me? I sat daily in the temple teaching, and you didn't arrest me. [56] But all this has happened that the Scriptures of the prophets might be fulfilled."

Then all the disciples left him and fled.

OBSERVATIONS

Jesus' security in the Father's love and purpose enabled Jesus to withstand all the attacks against Him without needing to resort to self-defence. He also shared the Father's love towards those at whose hands and for whom He was suffering. All I felt was fear........

42

CAIAPHAS

CONTEXT

Jesus consistently exercised a public ministry that included miracles that had never been seen before and that drew crowds who were hungry for healing and in awe of Jesus' power. His ministry also involved controversy with the religious leaders and a host of stories told at their expense, along with repeated Messianic claims that caused divisions of opinion about His true identity among the common people and religious leaders alike.

It was the week leading up to the Passover and Jesus was in Jerusalem with His disciples in order to celebrate the festival along with the rest of the population. The religious leaders were intent on arresting Jesus and finding a way to have Him killed. They finally succeeded in the arrest and were then in search of a charge to bring against Jesus, so that they could take Him to Pilate to request that He be executed.

MATTHEW 26:57-68

QUESTIONS FOR THOUGHT OR DISCUSSION

What was the law that the high priest and chief priests hoped to use to convict Jesus? (Leviticus 24:10-16)

What safeguards were in place in Jewish law to protect innocent victims? (Deuteronomy 19:15-21)

Why did the priests have difficulty in establishing their case?

What sins were involved in the attempt to convict Jesus?

What was holding the hearts of the high priest and chief priests captive?

What did the high priest and chief priests need to turn away from?

What would it have cost the high priest and chief priests to acclaim Jesus?

What would the high priest and chief priests have gained from turning to God and acknowledging Jesus?

Why did Jesus remain silent in the face of the charge against Him?

What question did Jesus answer and why?

What did Jesus say in answer to the high priest? (Daniel 7:13-14 and Psalm 110:1-2)

What do Jesus' reply and conduct tell us about Himself and Father God?

COMMENTS

As high priest, Caiaphas had everything going for him. He was capable, recognized, powerful. In spite of all that, Jesus presented him with a challenge. Jesus had power to heal people and to draw crowds, which indicated popularity with the people that Caiaphas lacked. Had Caiaphas really cared about the people being healed, one might have expected that he would be thrilled at what was happening in Jesus' ministry. He was not. He was more bothered about his own self-importance than about the welfare or success of others. Robbed of the limelight, he felt his power and authority threatened and wanted Jesus out of the way. Pure envy, which was not lost on Pilate. The chief priests were mostly of the same mind and together they exerted strong peer pressure on one another. To remain part of the club was all important. The alternative was social ostracism and exclusion from the worshipping community, all in the name of the one God they claimed to worship.

To hear Jesus proclaiming Himself to be that God was more than the chief priests could take. It meant that if He were telling the truth they had a lot of repenting to do. That would have come at a cost to their self-importance and they were not willing to pay the price. In response, they tried to silence Jesus instead. The truth about where their loyalty lay was exposed in their statement to Pilate that they had no king but Caesar, when Pilate wanted to release Jesus. This was the logical consequence of suggesting to Pilate that Jesus deserved to die because He had proclaimed Himself a king, thus putting Himself in opposition to Caesar. Anything to maintain their positions of authority within the status quo. The chief priests loved their lives in this world more than they loved God.

MEDITATION

Events around Jesus appear to be totally out of control. Or maybe totally under control, but the control of the wrong people. Jesus is now captive, only going where He is being taken by His captors. Back through the now deserted streets of Jerusalem. Up the long stone staircase to Caiaphas' house. Hardly able to see in the pitch darkness. Alone and deserted by all His friends. Unwilling to defend Himself.

> [57] Those who had taken Jesus led him away to Caiaphas the high priest, where the scribes and the elders were gathered together. [58] But Peter followed him from a distance to the court of the high priest, and entered in and sat with the officers, to see the end.

> [59] Now the chief priests, the elders, and the whole council sought false testimony against Jesus, that they might put him to death, [60] and they found none. Even though many false witnesses came forward, they found none. But at last two false witnesses came forward [61] and said, "This man said, 'I am able to destroy the temple of God, and to build it in three days.'"

> [62] The high priest stood up and said to him, "Have you no answer? What is this that these testify against you? [63] But Jesus stayed silent. The high priest answered him, "I adjure you by the living God that you tell us whether you are the Christ, the Son of God."

> [64] Jesus said to him, "You have said so. Nevertheless, I tell you, after this you will see the Son of Man sitting at the right hand of Power, and coming on the clouds of the sky."

> [65] Then the high priest tore his clothing, saying, "He has spoken blasphemy! Why do we need any more witnesses? Behold, now you have heard his blasphemy. [66] What do you think?"

They answered, "He is worthy of death!" ⁶⁷ Then they spat in his face and beat him with their fists, and some slapped him, ⁶⁸ saying, "Prophesy to us, you Christ! Who hit you?"

OBSERVATIONS

It is frightening to realize how easy it is to be very religious and at the same time so far from God and His love.

Jesus remained secure in His sense of identity and the knowledge of who He was. He also remained committed to letting people know who He was, so that the significance of His visit to earth would not be missed by the human race. He was utterly transparent and truthful, regardless of the cost involved. His reliance on the Father for vindication meant that He had no need to justify Himself. When put under oath, He told the truth even when He knew that it would cost Him His life. Had He not done so, not only would He have called the truth into question for all time, He would also have betrayed His integrity and not been fit to be a perfect and sufficient sacrifice for our sins.

Had the resurrection not vindicated Him, Jesus would indeed have deserved the charge of megalomania that the chief priests thought Him guilty of, but the resurrection did vindicate Him. He was utterly secure in the Father's love for Him and in His certainty that the Father would instate Him at His right hand while He put all His enemies under His feet. He made no attempt to manipulate those around Him in order to protect Himself, He left them free to make their own choices and loved them still.

43

PILATE

CONTEXT

Pilate was a Roman, a governor from an occupying force. The local Jewish puppet king, Archelaus, had proved exceptionally brutal and the Jews had complained about him to Rome. Rather than replace him, the Romans had decided on direct rule and the number one priority for Pilate was to keep the peace. If he failed to do that, he would have to answer to Caesar and the consequences for him could be grave. It was in that context that Pilate found himself confronted by the Jewish leaders, wanting him to authorize the execution of a fellow Jew, whom they had already taken prisoner. The Jews were not authorized by Rome to dispense capital punishment, they had to rely on the Roman authorities to make such decisions.

JOHN 18:33-38 and 19:4-16

QUESTIONS FOR THOUGHT OR DISCUSSION

What were the differences in world views between the Jews and Pilate?

Were there any similarities between the Jews and Pilate?

Why did the Jewish leaders want to have Jesus crucified?

What was Pilate's attitude to Jesus in verse 35?

What did Jesus give as His reason for being in the world in verse 37?

What did Pilate make of Jesus?

What did Jesus imply to Pilate in verse 11?

Why did Pilate not want to have Jesus crucified?

Why did Pilate go along with the Jewish leaders' request that he authorize Jesus' execution?

How did Jesus view Pilate?

COMMENTS

Naturally Pilate wanted to know what Jesus had done wrong. He received no satisfactory answer however, merely an assurance from the Jewish leaders that had Jesus not done anything wrong they would not have brought Jesus before him. To his credit, that was not good enough for Pilate, so he decided to question Jesus directly. He appears to have known that the Jews were accusing Jesus of making out that He was a king. Not being a Jew, Pilate would not have been interested in Jewish blasphemy laws, nor seen a breach of them as a capital offence. The accusation that Jesus claimed to be a king did not sound to Pilate to be worthy of capital punishment either, Jesus hardly looked a threat to Rome's authority. Hence Pilate's question to the Jewish leaders about what Jesus had done that was wrong. As Jesus' claim to kingship was the only accusation so far, Pilate questioned Jesus about it. Ever wanting to draw people out into self-awareness and integrity, Jesus asked Pilate whether he really believed that He was a king, or whether he was just repeating what others had told him. Pilate's reply made it clear that he did not believe it, he was merely quoting. Jesus then answered Pilate's question by explaining that He was not a king of this world and pointing out that if He were, His disciples would have fought to protect Him. From this Pilate concluded that Jesus was not really a king at all but was deluded. Hardly a crime worthy of death. Jesus could have let it rest there, but it would not have been true. It is difficult to see who stood to benefit from Jesus' response other than Pilate. Jesus pursued the kingship issue and explained that He was on earth to witness to the truth. Did He mean to Father God or the truth of who He was or both? Either way, Pilate was forced to face the fact that he did not understand and asked the question 'What is truth?' From a Jewish perspective he would have done better to ask, 'Who is truth?' but his perspective was quite different from that of the Jews. Although he did not understand their blasphemy laws, he was able to see, more clearly than the Jewish leaders, that Jesus had done nothing wrong that was worthy of death from a Roman perspective. He therefore determined to release Jesus.

Pilate was in the habit of releasing a convicted Jewish criminal once a year on the eve of the Passover. Although Jesus was neither convicted nor a criminal, Pilate sought to use this mechanism to release Jesus. The chief priests, however, asked Pilate to release Barabbas instead. When

Pilate had Jesus scourged and then paraded Jesus in front of the crowd, they shouted for Jesus to be crucified. Pilate refused, saying that he had not found any fault in Jesus. Whereupon the Jews informed him that they had a law that Jesus should die for making out that he was the Son of God. This struck fear into Pilate. He was caught between needing to keep the peace for Rome and wanting to execute justice for Jesus. He took Jesus back in for further questioning. Whence had He come? Pilate wanted to know. Jesus did not answer. Pilate reminded Jesus that he had authority to release Him or to have Him crucified. Jesus pointed out to Pilate that he would not have had any such authority had it not been granted to him from above and that those who were determined to use his authority to end His life were guiltier than Pilate. What a clever way to convict Pilate of sin on Jesus' part. Jesus was throughout maintaining his focus on integrity and truth. This comment from Jesus convinced Pilate to seek to let Jesus go. However, Pilate still needed to keep the Jews happy in order to keep Rome happy in order to keep himself safe. Suffering the consequences of acting justly was too high a price for Pilate to pay for doing the right thing by Jesus. The Jews knew just where to aim to bring Pilate round to honouring their request. If Jesus were a king, he could not be a friend of Caesar. Nor then could anyone else who supported Jesus.

Faced with such a dilemma, Pilate made one last attempt to showcase the issue. He brought Jesus out and said: "Behold, your King!" When the Jews continued to clamour for Jesus to be crucified, Pilate countered with: "Shall I crucify your King?" At that the Jewish leaders showed their true colours in protesting that they had no king but Caesar. Assimilation with the world, identification with the values of worldly authorities, caring more for their positions in society than for God all contributed to their rejection of Jesus and with Him, of God Himself. Their envy of Jesus led to a complete indifference to justice. Their number one priority was their own interests.

PILATE

MEDITATION

³³ Pilate therefore entered again into the Praetorium, called Jesus, and said to him, "Are you the King of the Jews?"

³⁴ Jesus answered him, "Do you say this by yourself, or did others tell you about me?"

³⁵ Pilate answered, "I'm not a Jew, am I? Your own nation and the chief priests delivered you to me. What have you done?"

³⁶ Jesus answered, "My Kingdom is not of this world. If my Kingdom were of this world, then my servants would fight, that I wouldn't be delivered to the Jews. But now my Kingdom is not from here."

³⁷ Pilate therefore said to him, "Are you a king then?"

Jesus answered, "You say that I am a king. For this reason I have been born, and for this reason I have come into the world, that I should testify to the truth. Everyone who is of the truth listens to my voice."

³⁸ Pilate said to him, "What is truth?"

When he had said this, he went out again to the Jews, and said to them, "I find no basis for a charge against him.

* * *

⁴ Then Pilate went out again, and said to them, "Behold, I bring him out to you, that you may know that I find no basis for a charge against him."

⁵ Jesus therefore came out, wearing the crown of thorns and the purple garment. Pilate said to them, "Behold, the man!"

⁶ When therefore the chief priests and the officers saw him, they shouted, saying, "Crucify! Crucify!"

Pilate said to them, "Take him yourselves, and crucify him, for I find no basis for a charge against him."

⁷ The Jews answered him, "We have a law, and by our law he ought to die, because he made himself the Son of God."

⁸ When therefore Pilate heard this saying, he was more afraid. ⁹ He entered into the Praetorium again, and said to Jesus, "Where are you from?" But Jesus gave him no answer. ¹⁰ Pilate therefore said to him, "Aren't you speaking to me? Don't you know that I have power to release you and have power to crucify you?"

¹¹ Jesus answered, "You would have no power at all against me, unless it were given to you from above. Therefore he who delivered me to you has greater sin."

¹² At this, Pilate was seeking to release him, but the Jews cried out, saying, "If you release this man, you aren't Caesar's friend! Everyone who makes himself a king speaks against Caesar!"

¹³ When Pilate therefore heard these words, he brought Jesus out and sat down on the judgment seat at a place called "The Pavement", but in Hebrew, "Gabbatha." ¹⁴ Now it was the Preparation Day of the Passover, at about the sixth hour. He said to the Jews, "Behold, your King!"

¹⁵ They cried out, "Away with him! Away with him! Crucify him!"

Pilate said to them, "Shall I crucify your King?"

The chief priests answered, "We have no king but Caesar!"

¹⁶ So then he delivered him to them to be crucified. So they took Jesus and led him away.

OBSERVATIONS

Jesus never lost His sense of identity, even when flogged and mocked by Pilate and his cohort of soldiers. Rather, Jesus continued throughout to exhibit His authority in the situation and to proclaim the truth, including about Pilate's sin and also that of the Jews. Jesus also relativised Pilate's position in the scheme of things, by referring to a higher authority than Caesar, without whose permission Pilate would have held no power over Jesus. It was not lost on Pilate that Jesus was different from any other prisoner that he had had dealings with; he sensed enough to feel afraid. But he had no faith with which to counteract his fear of a more immediate threat, that of losing his position. Self-protection trumped righteousness in Pilate's life.

Such choices continue to face all of us in today's world.

44

THE ROMAN SOLDIERS

CONTEXT
Pilate, against his better judgment, released Barabbas at the insistence of the crowd. He had Jesus flogged and then handed Him over to be crucified. It would appear that Jesus had a profile with the Romans, as the whole cohort of five hundred men turned out to make sport of Him.

THE ROMAN SOLDIERS

MATTHEW 27:27-31 and 50-54

QUESTIONS FOR THOUGHT OR DISCUSSION

What would the Roman soldiers have known about Jesus?

How would He have appeared to the Roman cohort having been sentenced and flogged?

Why did the Roman soldiers need to mock Jesus?

What injuries did the Roman soldiers inflict on Jesus?

What does the soldiers' behaviour tell us about human nature?

What would the impact of the soldiers' mockery have been on Jesus?

How did Father God respond to the mistreatment of Jesus?

What conclusion did the Roman centurion draw about Jesus when he had watched Jesus die?

What events contributed to the Roman centurion's conclusion?

How did the Roman centurion end up feeling?

Do the events surrounding Jesus' death that were witnessed by the centurion influence your view about how Father God responded to the situation?

What can we conclude about Jesus and Father God?

COMMENTS

Jesus told His disciples, in advance of the event, that He was going to be mocked during His trial in Jerusalem. The psychological impact must have been pretty devastating. There is no reference to how Jesus responded, suggesting that He held His tongue with dignity. Maybe He was forearmed by being forewarned. Maybe He was so aware of the realities of human nature that it was no surprise to find Himself on the receiving end of such mockery.

Why was it that the Roman soldiers needed to go through the process of mocking Jesus? Was it that they could not resist giving vent to their disparagement, faced with a country carpenter in an occupied territory who apparently imagined Himself to be a king? Anyone as deluded as that had to be pitied, nay despised even, for His mental derangement. Or was it that, trained to kill as they were, the soldiers still needed to assuage their guilt in some way when faced with the job of killing someone whom they knew to be innocent. Puffing up their self-importance at the expense of an insignificant minion might have seemed to justify that they had the right to dictate the outcome, or at least collude with it in the process of obeying orders. Or was it, for most of them, simply the need to maintain solidarity with one another? Their own lives could be at the mercy of their fellow soldiers if in need of help on the battlefield or during the frequent riots that they had to quell. Peer group solidarity was essential to their chances of survival. Jesus was an outsider and a supposed threat to the status quo and as such a common enemy. Or maybe they were just bored and caricaturing Him according to the charge against Him provided them with some momentary sport and the chance to exercise a semblance of power, beating Him over the head with a staff. How many other times had Jesus felt belittled by the responses from people who did not recognize who He was? What has that felt like and what does it feel like still? He certainly made no attempt to impose His authority or control people's responses to Him. He simply held His peace and left the outcome to His Father.

The Father was eerily silent throughout the trial and crucifixion, to the point where Jesus eventually cried out asking why He had been forsaken so completely. Right up until the moment He died, apparently. Then there was an immediate earthquake, the veil in the Temple was torn from top to bottom, the rocks were rent, tombs were opened, and the dead raised after Jesus' resurrection. The Roman centurion probably would not have been aware of what was happening in the Temple, nor particularly impacted by the significance of it, that was more of a message for the Jews. However, he was impacted by the earthquake, to the point where he completely revised his view of the plausibility of Jesus' claim to be a king with the comment: "Truly this was the Son of God." Even as a non-Jew it would appear that he could recognize the Father speaking out in vindication of His Son through abnormal and earth-shattering events.

MEDITATION

It is the eve of Passover. The Roman cohort are up early, as usual, ready to patrol the heaving streets of Jerusalem and to quell any riots that might threaten to develop. Jewish festivals are not exactly routine days, although they come round with irritating regularity. Still, Rome is perfectly able to cope, they have the upper hand in this unruly province and that is how they intend it to continue. This day is starting to look slightly different however, as word is going round the garrison that the controversial figure, Jesus, is in custody. A rare opportunity is presenting itself to take a close-up view of what He is really like. And they are being called out, leaving no choice as to their response.

> [27] Then the governor's soldiers took Jesus into the Praetorium, and gathered the whole garrison together against him. [28] They stripped him and put a scarlet robe on him. [29] They braided a crown of thorns and put it on his head, and a reed in his right hand; and they kneeled down before him and mocked him, saying, "Hail, King of the Jews!" [30] They spat on him, and took the reed and struck him on the head. [31] When they had mocked him, they took the robe off him, and put his clothes on him, and led him away to crucify him.

* * *

⁵⁰ Jesus cried again with a loud voice, and yielded up his spirit.

⁵¹ Behold, the veil of the temple was torn in two from the top to the bottom. The earth quaked and the rocks were split. ⁵² The tombs were opened, and many bodies of the saints who had fallen asleep were raised; ⁵³ and coming out of the tombs after his resurrection, they entered into the holy city and appeared to many.

⁵⁴ Now the centurion and those who were with him watching Jesus, when they saw the earthquake and the things that were done, were terrified, saying, "Truly this was the Son of God!"

OBSERVATIONS

Watching the soldiers felt very uncomfortable and produced a feeling of anxiety. They were trapped in a system in which they were required to do whatever was asked of them, including in this case murdering an innocent man in a very cruel way. To opt out was to risk one's own life, which was exactly what Jesus had said was required of anyone aspiring to become His disciple.

45

JOHN AND MARY, THE MOTHER OF JESUS

CONTEXT

According to John's Gospel, Pilate handed Jesus over to be crucified on the eve of the Passover. Jesus had not been in custody for long and sentencing took place at the earliest possible moment. John followed all the events and was well placed to be keeping the women informed about what was happening. Jesus' mother Mary, along with her sister Salome, who was probably John's mother, plus Mary's sister-in-law Mary and a friend, also called Mary were all standing together very close to the cross as Jesus was crucified. Alone among the disciples John, who was probably Jesus' cousin, was close by. Nine of the disciples appear to have fled Jerusalem following Jesus' arrest. Jesus' brothers were nowhere to be seen.

JOHN 19:25-27

QUESTIONS FOR THOUGHT OR DISCUSSION

In what ways was Mary's life impacted by being the mother of Jesus?

Is that what you might have anticipated for someone described by the angel as blessed?

What does to be blessed really mean?

Do you think that the Western Church fails to accurately portray the meaning of blessedness and if so, how?

In what ways does John stand out from the other disciples and Jesus' brothers?

What risks was John taking to be present at the crucifixion, which may not have applied to the women?

Do you think that John's love for Jesus might have been why he felt himself to be "the disciple whom Jesus loved?" (John 19:26)

What difference would it have made for Mary had she not been within earshot of Jesus at the crucifixion?

What difference would it have made for Jesus had John not been there?

What must it have cost Jesus to send Mary and John from the scene?

What does Jesus' care for Mary tell us about Father God's heart?

COMMENTS
Mary risked her entire future to say yes to God and carry Jesus. What must it have been like to be watching Jesus robbed of His future? Hopefully she remembered Simeon's prophecy that a sword would pierce her own heart, as the unexpected is never as bad when we know it has been predicted and therefore that God is not being taken by surprise. We are not told, and it might have only been later that it was brought to mind by events.

How could such a tragedy and travesty of justice possibly be in line with God's purposes? Mary's love for Jesus meant that she wanted to support Him until the end, and needed to know what happened to Him, so she was present near the cross, along with her sister, sister-in-law and a friend. They had come with her nephew John, described in his Gospel as the one whom Jesus loved, who was standing not very far away. Mary and the others did not need to say anything, their very presence must have been a source of comfort and support to Jesus, however much He might have wanted to protect His mother and maybe also Himself from what she was going through on His account. She had been called blessed by the angel who appeared to her to announce the coming of Jesus, but such blessedness had come at a cost in a number of ways during the course of her life. As well as having the privilege of watching at close hand Jesus grow and develop and the activities that He undertook, she suffered lifelong reputational damage in connection with Jesus' assumed illegitimacy, refugee status in Egypt, displacement from Bethlehem to Nazareth, the rejection of Jesus by the people of Nazareth and fear of the authorities through being associated with Jesus when His ministry proved politically dangerous. Now the ultimate nightmare, to watch her son die the unjust and public death of a criminal. Blessedness or happiness is not a feeling, it is a function of our standing before God in a world that mostly stands against Him.

We are left to conclude that Jesus' brothers had run away on hearing of His fate. Their attitude to Jesus when they had tried to interrupt His ministry and again when they taunted Him about attending a Jerusalem festival suggests that there was not much love for Him on their parts. What would it have been like for Mary to go home and hear their callous chat about the word on the street, just when she would most be needing support in her grief?

In spite of His own agony, Mary's presence and her needs were not lost on Jesus and He was concerned to provide for her welfare and not to leave her potentially destitute. He was also concerned to protect her from spending the next few hours watching Him die, something that she could do without having etched into her memory for the rest of her life. To protect Mary, Jesus had to suffer her early departure from the scene and had to rely on the assistance of the only disciple present, John. He was the only male member of the group, that Jesus had previously indicated He viewed as His true family, still within earshot. Jesus knew that John would share Mary's grief at His death and be able to offer her genuine support. The fact that John was present at the crucifixion meant that he was within earshot when Jesus needed to appeal to him for help for Mary. The fact that Mary was within earshot too meant that she knew that to allow John to take her home with him was acceptable. In fact as Mary's nephew, John was the best placed person to adopt Mary into his family. Seeing them go must have been costly for Jesus, even though it would have saved Him from witnessing His mother's suffering.

Three days later John would be one of the first disciples to see the evidence of the resurrection and to believe it. Mary would have been within earshot of the news at the earliest possible moment, by being within John's household. She would also have been well placed to hear of subsequent events, when Jesus appeared repeatedly to His followers, and would have been protected from rumours and the lies put round by the authorities and the hurt and confusion that that would have caused her, listening to her other sons repeating the Jerusalem gossip. Jesus so knew what Mary needed and her being in His presence resulted in her receiving His provision for her.

MEDITATION

Amongst the crowd of mockers and scoffers, standing close to the hardened and indifferent Roman soldiers, who are helping themselves to Jesus' clothes, stands a small group of people who are genuinely heartbroken by what is happening to Jesus. They are powerless to protect Him, but they refuse to desert Him. It might be dangerous to be there and seen to care, but they do not want to leave, even though the pain and distress are unbearable, especially for Mary, watching her first-born die an ignominious and unjust public death. She must be feeling as though she is dying on the inside.

> [25] But standing by Jesus' cross were his mother, his mother's sister, Mary the wife of Clopas, and Mary Magdalene. [26] Therefore when Jesus saw his mother, and the disciple whom he loved standing there, he said to his mother, "Woman, behold, your son!" [27] Then he said to the disciple, "Behold, your mother!" From that hour, the disciple took her to his own home.

OBSERVATIONS

John would probably have felt that he could have been risking his own life, being present at Jesus' crucifixion. Nevertheless he loved Jesus enough to disregard that and stay close. It meant that he was within earshot when Jesus wanted help for His mother. That God would make Himself dependent on human beings for His own needs and those of His human family is a sobering thought. That John heard what Jesus wanted help with and responded with obedience to a request that had lifetime implications is a challenging example of what discipleship involves.

46

THE CRIMINALS CRUCIFIED WITH JESUS

CONTEXT

It is very likely that John is the only Gospel writer whose account of Jesus' death is first hand, reflecting the fact that he was there at the time and witnessed it. However, John does not record Jesus' conversation with the criminal in his Gospel. It is possible that he took Mary back to her sister Salome's house as soon as Jesus asked him to take care of Mary as his mother. He may well have stayed with her for a while, to make sure that she was going to be alright. Then he returned to the scene of the crucifixion in time to hear the last few words that Jesus uttered. We therefore have to rely on Luke for a record of the interaction between

THE CRIMINALS CRUCIFIED WITH JESUS

Jesus and those on the crosses either side of Him.

LUKE 23:32-43

QUESTIONS FOR THOUGHT OR DISCUSSION

What might the criminals who were crucified with Jesus have been thinking and feeling on their way to being crucified?

How might it have felt for Jesus to be crucified between two criminals?

Where was the focus of Jesus' attention?

What was the significance of the comment about the Roman soldiers casting lots for Jesus' clothes? (Psalm 22:18)

Why did the rulers and soldiers feel the need to sneer?

How would you describe the heart of the first criminal to speak to Jesus on the cross?

How would you describe the attitude of the second criminal to speak?

What set the two criminals apart from each other?

What does Jesus' response to the second criminal tell us about both Himself and Father God?

COMMENTS

Passing by, outside the city wall, a stranger to Jerusalem travelling along the road in front of the three crosses might have been forgiven for assuming that they were witnessing the rightful crucifixion of three criminals, but for the fact that one of them had an unusual sign above His head proclaiming: "THIS IS THE KING OF THE JEWS." Maybe He was deranged. There was no shortage of mockery being aimed at Jesus on the part of the Jewish rulers and Roman soldiers, tempting Him to prove His identity by saving Himself. To make matters worse for Jesus, one of the criminals hanging beside Him took up the theme. The snippets of conversation between the criminals and Jesus, into which Luke gives us a brief window, must have been punctuated by gasps for breath and groans of pain. The criminals may have been Zealots who had been involved in the recent insurrection led by Barabbas. The first criminal to speak showed no respect for Jesus, whom he may well have considered to be a failed leader who had lost sight of the cause. While Jesus was focussed on the Father, the criminal was focussed on the overthrow of Rome. He was blasphemous and just wanted Jesus to save both of them. He found himself being roundly rebuked by the other criminal in a quite remarkable series of comments, not what one might expect from a criminal. In a few short words, the second criminal indicated a respect for God and a recognition that he could not point the finger when he was rightly convicted. Furthermore he demonstrated an acceptance of responsibility for his crime, an acceptance of his punishment as deserved and an acknowledgement that Jesus did not deserve what was being meted out to Him as He had done nothing wrong. And then in a declaration of belief in Jesus' kingship he asked to be remembered by Jesus when He came into His Kingdom. This indicates a criminal with a humble and contrite heart. Not only that, but he also displayed an acceptance of mortality and a belief in Jesus' ability to reverse it beyond the grave. It was a statement of faith, to which Jesus was quick to respond with an assurance that his request would be granted. Nothing more was needed from the second criminal for him to receive Jesus' total acceptance. In fact he was to be the first person to enter Jesus' Kingdom, a clear message that Jesus' Kingdom is open to those who do not deserve to enter it.

THE CRIMINALS CRUCIFIED WITH JESUS

MEDITATION

Out of imprisonment, but what for? To carry an instrument of execution through the streets, past the crowds and out of the city to a well-known vantage point. This is it then, no chance of a reprieve now. Death looms. How unjust. Life has never been fair. Now there is nothing left but to rail against this unfair world. Powerlessness, despair, rage. Honesty, responsibility, submission. Other centred compassion and forgiveness.

[32] There were also others, two criminals, led with him to be put to death. [33] When they came to the place that is called "The Skull", they crucified him there with the criminals, one on the right and the other on the left.

[34] Jesus said, "Father, forgive them, for they don't know what they are doing."

Dividing his garments among them, they cast lots. [35] The people stood watching. The rulers with them also scoffed at him, saying, "He saved others. Let him save himself, if this is the Christ of God, his chosen one!"

[36] The soldiers also mocked him, coming to him and offering him vinegar, [37] and saying, "If you are the King of the Jews, save yourself!"

[38] An inscription was also written over him in letters of Greek, Latin, and Hebrew: "THIS IS THE KING OF THE JEWS."

[39] One of the criminals who was hanged insulted him, saying, "If you are the Christ, save yourself and us!"

[40] But the other answered, and rebuking him said, "Don't you even fear God, seeing you are under the same condemnation? [41] And we indeed justly, for we receive the due reward for our deeds, but this

man has done nothing wrong." ⁴²He said to Jesus, "Lord, remember me when you come into your Kingdom."

⁴³ Jesus said to him, "Assuredly I tell you, today you will be with me in Paradise."

OBSERVATIONS

The injustice of the situation was huge and the temptation to prove His identity by succumbing to the incessant taunts must have been immense for Jesus. At no point did He give in. Instead He trusted the Father implicitly to vindicate Him in His own good time. I found myself getting really angry at the injustice and feeling challenged about my lack of trust. Jesus displayed no anger whatever, only acceptance of the people around Him in all their sinfulness and a desire for the Father to forgive.

47

MARY MAGDALENE AND THE OTHER MARY MEET THE RISEN JESUS

CONTEXT

Jesus was dead. His body was no longer moving. He was limp; but becoming stiff. Dusk was approaching. The women should go home. But they could not leave. The bottom had dropped out of their world. They did not know what to do. There was nothing left to do. They needed to know what would happen to Jesus' body.

MATTHEW 27:57-61 and 28:1-10

QUESTIONS FOR THOUGHT OR DISCUSSION

What risks did Joseph of Arimathea take in going to Pilate to request Jesus' body?

Why might Joseph have felt that it was important to remove Jesus' body from the cross? (Deuteronomy 21:22-23)

What theological significance was implied by the placing of Jesus' body in Joseph's tomb? (Isaiah 53:9)

What practical difference did it make that Jesus' body was placed in a tomb, rather than in a mass grave, thinking ahead to the resurrection?

What custom might Mary Magdalene and the other Mary have been following in visiting Jesus' tomb?

What were the obstacles that Mary Magdalene and the other Mary faced?

Why had the Roman soldiers been posted at the tomb?

Would you describe any of the women's intentions and actions as prayer?

How was the women's devotion to Jesus repaid?

What does this tell us about the Father heart of God?

COMMENTS

It is difficult to imagine what the women thought they were waiting for. Normally Jesus' body would have been left hanging on the cross for a while yet. In fact normally He would not be dead yet. Once He was, the Romans would have dumped his body unceremoniously in a mass tomb reserved for the executed.[2] They would not have been worried about doing so on a Sabbath, although they did break the legs of people to hasten their deaths if they wanted to remove their bodies before sunset. None of that proved necessary for Jesus. Suddenly a Jewish leader, whom the women would have recognized as Joseph, appeared, accompanied by a group of Roman soldiers and possibly some servants. More soldiers. What was happening? Hauling the cross into place was one thing, winching it down again not an option. The Romans rarely removed empty crosses, they were everywhere, reminding people who was in charge. Being present to Jesus' body being taken off the cross would have been gruelling. The women might well have felt sick watching. Joseph and his servants were there, ready with a cloth. It is likely that they wrapped the body of Jesus in it with a gentleness not characteristic of Roman soldiers. The women might well have been bemused. Was it not the Jewish leaders who had incited the crowd to yell for Jesus to be crucified? Joseph appeared to be different. But what would he do next? The women felt so out of control. All they could do, as ever, was watch. Joseph's servants picked Jesus' body up and set off, away from the crosses, on two of which the inert bodies of the criminals continued to hang. The Roman soldiers followed Joseph and his servants. The women followed the soldiers. Down a stony track to a wild and deserted area not far away, outside the city, a low cliff in which a number of tombs had been hewn. One of them was newly hewn and belonged to Joseph. They watched as Joseph's servants placed the body of Jesus on the ground and rolled back the stone covering the mouth of the tomb. Then the servants entered with the body and reappeared without it. They rolled the stone across the tomb and departed. The Roman soldiers stayed. The women just sat there. They did not know for how long. They did not want to leave.

Eventually the impending Sabbath required that they make their way home before it got dark. At least they knew where to go when the Sabbath was over and it was time to anoint Jesus' body with spices, according to the custom of allowing a couple of days to elapse before checking that death had in fact taken place. Not normally possible for crucified criminals, whose bodies were routinely thrown into a mass grave. Not even really necessary. Although checking on Jesus' body was possible, because He was in a tomb, the women would have known that Jesus was already proven dead. Roman centurions knew how to certify death; had they not plunged a sword into Jesus' side to check? The horror of it. The women had seen it all. Still they wanted to anoint Jesus' body with spices.

As soon as it was daylight after the Sabbath, the women were heading back to the tomb with their spices. Who was going to roll back the stone? The Roman soldiers were still there. How were the women going to be able to do what they had come for? Suddenly the ground started shaking and an apparition appeared, like lightening, dazzling white and larger than life. The soldiers were terrified and became lifeless. The angel rolled back the stone and sat on it. The women were terrified too, but the angel answered their unspoken question:

> "Don't be afraid, for I know that you seek Jesus, who has been crucified.
>
> ⁶ He is not here, for he has risen, just like he said. Come, see the place where the Lord was lying."

It was cold and gloomy inside the tomb. They would have had to crawl through a low and narrow entrance tunnel before being able to stand up again once inside. They could just make out the shelf with the cloth lying flat and empty. It was a previously unused tomb. There was no body. They came back out again quickly; they did not want to become trapped inside. The angel was still speaking:

⁷ "Go quickly and tell his disciples, 'He has risen from the dead, and behold, he goes before you into Galilee; there you will see him.' Behold, I have told you."

The women rushed off, feeling terrified and joyful all at once. They were running to tell the disciples when who should they bump into but Jesus! When He spoke to them His voice was utterly recognizable. They fell at His feet, a common sign of subordination in that culture, worshipping Him and heard him telling them not to be afraid, just to go and tell His brothers, meaning the disciples, to leave for Galilee, where they would see Him.

MEDITATION

⁵⁷ When evening had come, a rich man from Arimathaea named Joseph, who himself was also Jesus' disciple, came. ⁵⁸ This man went to Pilate and asked for Jesus' body. Then Pilate commanded the body to be given up. ⁵⁹ Joseph took the body and wrapped it in a clean linen cloth ⁶⁰ and laid it in his own new tomb, which he had cut out in the rock. Then he rolled a large stone against the door of the tomb, and departed. ⁶¹ Mary Magdalene was there, and the other Mary, sitting opposite the tomb.

It has been a long Sabbath. Empty. A Passover not to be remembered. Nothing for it but to be at the Temple, confined to the Court of Women. The teaching has seemed empty, meaningless, applicable only to the men. How could it apply, women do not count as people. Jesus was so different. He showed respect and appreciation for your care of Him. And now He is gone. What has gone wrong? Where is Yahweh? Does He not care? What is the point of life now? Who is there left to care for? Who will appreciate us now?

At last, the first day of the week. Dawn is breaking. It will be safe to set out very soon, with the customary spices, prepared before the Sabbath began. At last, time to anoint Jesus' body. Who will roll away the stone? Impossible to do on our own. And the guards. They are not normally posted outside tombs. Why are they here? Will they roll the stone back or deny entry? Are we women even safe to be here?

> 28 Now after the Sabbath, as it began to dawn on the first day of the week, Mary Magdalene and the other Mary came to see the tomb. ² Behold, there was a great earthquake, for an angel of the Lord descended from the sky and came and rolled away the stone from the door and sat on it. ³ His appearance was like lightning, and his clothing white as snow. ⁴ For fear of him, the guards shook, and became like dead men. ⁵ The angel answered the women, "Don't be afraid, for I know that you seek Jesus, who has been crucified. ⁶ He is not here, for he has risen, just like he said. Come, see the place where the Lord was lying. ⁷ Go quickly and tell his disciples, 'He has risen from the dead, and behold, he goes before you into Galilee; there you will see him.' Behold, I have told you."
>
> ⁸ They departed quickly from the tomb with fear and great joy, and ran to bring his disciples word. ⁹ As they went to tell his disciples, behold, Jesus met them, saying, "Rejoice!"
>
> They came and took hold of his feet, and worshiped him.
>
> ¹⁰ Then Jesus said to them, "Don't be afraid. Go tell my brothers that they should go into Galilee, and there they will see me."

OBSERVATIONS

All but one of the disciples had deserted or denied Jesus following His arrest, in order to save their own skins. Yet Jesus still referred to them as His brothers when He sent them His message via the two Marys. What a revelation to realize that previous disobedience on my part need not continue to cause a sense of break in my relationship with Jesus. What mercy!

ABOUT THE AUTHOR

JANE ATKINSON spent her childhood in Bristol, where she attended an evangelical, Anglican church. She discovered the power of Jesus to forgive sin and bring transformation as a teenager. After completing a degree in Soil Science and Biochemistry in Bangor, North Wales, where she worshipped in a Calvinist Chapel, she was a novice with the Anglican Sisters of Charity for four years, where she was introduced to Catholicism. The result was a lasting passion for Theology. Alongside working as a qualified hospital social worker in Sheffield, she completed a post-graduate diploma in the Theological Understanding of Industrial Society at Hull University and later a Masters in Theology at York St John. Having also completed a post-graduate certificate in Learning and Teaching she took up a lecturing post in Social Work at Sheffield Hallam University. She is now retired and living in Bristol, where she has enjoyed further theological study at Trinity Theological College.

Jane can be contacted online at https://www.persistentpilgrims.com

Thank you for reading! If you have benefitted from using this book please would you leave a review, as it will help others to find the book.

NOTES

PART 1: JESUS AND FATHER GOD

Session 1. Jesus' Baptism: pages 13-18

1. Jean-Pierre Isbouts, *In the Footsteps of Jesus* (Washington, D.C. National Geographic 2017), p. 84.

2. Jean-Pierre Isbouts, *In the Footsteps of Jesus* (Washington, D.C. National Geographic 2017), p. 117.

3. Jean-Pierre Isbouts, *In the Footsteps of Jesus* (Washington, D.C. National Geographic 2017), p. 149.

4. Jean-Pierre Isbouts, *In the Footsteps of Jesus* (Washington, D.C. National Geographic 2017), p. 150.

Session 3. Raising of Lazarus: pages 26–32

5. C. M. Pilkington, *Teach Yourself Judaism* (London, Hodder Headline Plc 1995), p. 169.

6. Jean-Pierre Isbouts, *In the Footsteps of Jesus* (Washington, D.C. National Geographic 2017), p. 223.

NOTES

Session 4. Jesus' Prayer for His Followers: pages 33–38

7. Colin J. Humphreys, *The Mystery of the Last Supper* (Cambridge University Press 2011), pp. 166-168.

Session 5. Jesus in Gethsemane: pages 39–45

8. Jean-Pierre Isbouts, *In the Footsteps of Jesus* (Washington, D.C. National Geographic 2017), p. 242.

9. Colin J. Humphreys, *The Mystery of the Last Supper* (Cambridge University Press 2011), p. 175.

Session 6. Death of Jesus: pages 46–52

10. Colin J. Humphreys, *The Mystery of the Last Supper* (Cambridge University Press 2011), p. 84.

PART 2: JESUS AND FAMILY

Session 7. Jesus' Parents when He was Twelve Years Old: pages 55–60

1. Jean-Pierre Isbouts, *In the Footsteps of Jesus* (Washington, D.C. National Geographic 2017), p. 84.

2. Jean-Pierre Isbouts, *In the Footsteps of Jesus* (Washington, D.C. National Geographic 2017), p. 115.

NOTES

3. Jean-Pierre Isbouts, *In the Footsteps of Jesus* (Washington, D.C. National Geographic 2017), p. 118.

4. Jean-Pierre Isbouts, *In the Footsteps of Jesus* (Washington, D.C. National Geographic 2017), p. 116.

Session 8. Jesus' Second Cousin, John the Baptist: pages 61–65

5. Jean-Pierre Isbouts, *In the Footsteps of Jesus* (Washington, D.C. National Geographic 2017), p. 142.

Session 12. Mary, the Mother of Jesus, at the Cross: pages 81–85

6. John Wenham, *Easter Enigma* (Exeter, The Paternoster Press 1984), pp. 40-41.

7. John Wenham, *Easter Enigma* (Exeter, The Paternoster Press 1984), pp. 28-33.

8. John Wenham, *Easter Enigma* (Exeter, The Paternoster Press 1984), p. 62.

PART 3: JESUS AND HIS DISCIPLES

Session 13. "Save Us, Lord! We Are Dying!": pages 89–93

1. John Wenham, *Easter Enigma* (Exeter, The Paternoster Press 1984), p. 40.

NOTES

Session 18. "Lord, How Often Shall My Brother Sin Against Me, and I Forgive Him?": pages 118–122

2. Corrie ten Boom, *The Hiding Place* (London, Hodder and Stoughton and Christian Literature Crusade 1973), pp. 220-221.

Session 21. "How Did the Fig Tree Immediately Wither Away?": pages 133–139

3. Tom Wright, *Matthew for Everyone Part 2, 2ⁿᵈ ed* (London, SPCK 2004), p. 72.

4. Tom Wright, *Matthew for Everyone Part 2, 2ⁿᵈ ed* (London, SPCK 2004), p. 71.

PART 4: JESUS AND THE SICK AND NEEDY

Session 25. Jairus's Daughter Raised from the Dead and a Woman's Haemorrhage Healed: pages 158–161

1. *The NIV Study Bible,* (London, Hodder & Stoughton Ltd 1987), p.1472.

Session 29. The Raising of Lazarus: pages 180–186

2. Jean-Pierre Isbouts, *In the Footsteps of Jesus* (Washington, D.C. National Geographic 2017), p. 223.

NOTES

PART 5: JESUS AND RELIGIOUS LEADERS

Session 30. Leave Home and Family: pages 189–193

1. Tom Wright, *Matthew for Everyone Part 1, 2nd ed* (London, SPCK 2004), p. 87.

Session 35. Divorce: pages 214–218

2. Donald A. Hagner, *World Biblical Commentary 33b Matthew 14-28* (Nashville, Dallas, Mexico City, Rio de Janeiro, Thomas Nelson Inc 1995), p. 547.

3. Donald A. Hagner, *World Biblical Commentary 33b Matthew 14-28* (Nashville, Dallas, Mexico City, Rio de Janeiro, Thomas Nelson Inc 1995), p. 549.

Session 37. Payment of Taxes: pages 225–229

4. Tom Wright, *Matthew for Everyone Part 2, 2nd ed* (London, SPCK 2004), p. 87.

5. Tom Wright, *Matthew for Everyone Part 2, 2nd ed* (London, SPCK 2004), pp. 87-88.

6. Tom Wright, *Matthew for Everyone Part 2, 2nd ed* (London, SPCK 2004), p. 88.

Session 39. The Great Commandment: pages 234–238

7. Donald A. Hagner, *World Biblical Commentary 33b Matthew 14-28* (Nashville, Dallas, Mexico City, Rio de Janeiro, Thomas Nelson Inc 1995), p. 646.

NOTES

PART 6: JESUS, THE CIVIC AUTHORITIES AND THE CROSS

Session 41. Judas: pages 248–253

1. Donald A. Hagner, *World Biblical Commentary 33b Matthew 14-28* (Nashville, Dallas, Mexico City, Rio de Janeiro, Thomas Nelson Inc 1995), p. 789.

Session 47. Mary Magdalene and the Other Mary Meet the Risen Jesus: pages 281–286

2. Jean-Pierre Isbouts, *In the Footsteps of Jesus* (Washington, D.C. National Geographic 2017), p. 266.